The Wit and Wisdom of
John Dewey

The Wit and Wisdom

of

John Dewey

Edited, with an Introduction, by

A. H. JOHNSON

PROFESSOR OF PHILOSOPHY
THE UNIVERSITY OF WESTERN ONTARIO
LONDON, CANADA

GREENWOOD PRESS, PUBLISHERS
NEW YORK

CONTENTS

PREFACE vii
ACKNOWLEDGMENTS ix
INTRODUCTION 3
KEY TO THE ABBREVIATIONS 44

THE WIT AND WISDOM OF JOHN DEWEY . . . . . .
  Philosophy and Philosophers 47
  Thinking 58
  Science 70
  Facts and Values 74
  Morality 78
  Art 84
  Religion 87
  Social Philosophy 89
  Education 102

PREFACE

John Dewey is the author of lengthy and technical studies of most of the major problems which confront the mind of man. It is interesting to note that even his enthusiastic followers sometimes forget that he is capable of expressing profound insights with sparkling and impressive brevity and clarity. Further it is easy to overlook the quiet, deep wit of New England which gleams in the midst of his most serious discussions.

This book is an attempt to provide a sample of John Dewey's wit and aphorismic wisdom. It takes the form of a series of quotations arranged under major topic headings. In each case the source has been indicated so that the interested reader may examine the context from which the selection is taken. Inevitably editorial "blind-spots" and preferences shape a process of selection. However many of Dewey's most frequently quoted statements are included in this compilation.

The Introductory Essay, which precedes the selections, outlines Dewey's general point of view. This, it is hoped, will facilitate the full understanding and appreciation of the quotations. A brief sketch of John Dewey's life and personality has been included for the same reason.

Here, then, is an introduction to the life and work of one of the most influential men of our time. It is designed to provide for the general reader a sample of the non-technical method of expression which John Dewey uses to enlighten and encourage men of intelligence and good will.

A. H. J.

ACKNOWLEDGMENTS

The following publishers and editors have kindly granted permission. to quote: The Beacon Press from *Reconstruction in Philosophy;* Blackie and Son from *Educational Essays;* E. P. Dutton and Company from *Schools of Tomorrow;* D. C. Heath and Company from *How We Think;* Henry Holt and Company from *Character and Events, Ethics, German Philosophy and Politics, Human Nature and Conduct, The Influence of Darwin on Philosophy, Intelligence in the Modern World, Logic: The Theory of Inquiry, The Philosophy of John Dewey, The Public and Its Problems;* Liveright Publishing Corporation from *The Sources of a Science of Education;* Longmans, Green and Company from *Whither Mankind;* The Macmillan Company from *Contemporary American Philosophy, Democracy and Education;* Minton, Balch and Company from *Art as Experience, Individualism Old and New, Philosophy and Civilization, The Quest for Certainty;* Open Court Publishing Company from *Experience and Nature;* Philosophical Library from *Problems of Men;* G. P. Putnam's Sons from *Education Today, Freedom and Culture, Liberalism and Social Action;* Simon and Schuster from *Living Philosophies;* the Editors of *Time;* The University of Chicago Press from *Essays in Experimental Logic, International Encyclopedia of Unified Science, The School and Society;* The Viking Press from *Philosopher's Holiday;* Yale University Press from *A Common Faith;* Dr. P. A. Schilpp, Editor, The Library of Living Philosophers, from *The Philosophy of John Dewey.*

I am very grateful to Professor Dewey for his permission to undertake this project, to Melvin Arnold for suggesting and facilitating it in every possible way; and to my wife for her assistance in preparing the manuscript.

A. H. J.

The Wit and Wisdom of
John Dewey

Introduction

SOME MEN EXEMPLIFY the best in their culture. A few point beyond to better things. John Dewey does both. His vigorous advocacy of the application of scientific attitudes and methods to all problems has greatly aided progressive tendencies on this continent and elsewhere. As a result of the thoughtful action of this man, his fellows have had a better opportunity to live and grow in a satisfying environment. Thereby many have achieved richness of experience. In the fields of education, politics, art, religion, and philosophy, John Dewey has laid foundations on which successive generations may well build a civilization which is the actualization of our sanest dreams.

John Dewey was born on October 20, 1859, at Burlington, Vermont. His father was a storekeeper whose interest in books was greater than his concern for the petty details of business. The influence of Dewey's mother was a decisive factor in turning him toward higher education and the world beyond Vermont. He grew up in a community where even small boys had definite responsibilities. Each member of the family had duties which must be performed if the welfare of all was to be attained. Children learned to rely on their own powers and initiative both at home and in the beautiful surrounding countryside. The impressive combination of sturdy independence and willingness to co-operate with others, which is so characteristic of John Dewey, is an unmistakable product of his early environment.

The class of 1879 at the University of Vermont was offered a rather restricted course of studies. Nevertheless, as he advanced toward graduation Dewey came upon several ideas which aroused intense interest—ideas which are fundamental in his thinking. In general, the kindly stimulus of Professor H. A. P. Torrey opened his eyes to the possibilities of a professional career in philosophy. At this time he acquired the knowledge of philosophic classics which is such an important factor in his work. The college library placed at his disposal such British journals as *The Fortnightly, The Nineteenth Century, The Contemporary Review.* Through these media Dewey became more fully aware of the intellectual ferments of his time—in particular, the impact of the natural sciences upon traditional points of view in every field of knowledge.

He derived from a study of the physiological writings of T. H. Huxley a notion of the unity of things. Later, referring to this experience, he said:

It is difficult to speak with exactitude about what happened to me intellectually so many years ago, but I have an impression that there was derived from that study a sense of interdependence and interrelated unity that gave form to intellectual stirrings that had been previously inchoate, and created a kind of type or model of a view of things to which material in any field ought to conform.[1]

Auguste Comte's Positivism focused his attention on the possibility of a scientific approach to social problems, and, in general, the relation between ideas and social environment. This interest tended to absorb time and energy which many of his contemporaries devoted to religious thinking. It is important to note that although Dewey's abandonment of traditional creeds and institutions involved a trying personal crisis, the basis of this transition was personal experience rather than the impact of any philosophic theory. The name of William James is given an honored place in the list of those to whom Dewey acknowledges intellectual indebtedness. *The Principles of Psychology* emphasized, among other themes, the importance of a biological approach to psychological data. This vital (rather than mechanistic) biology, involving a stress on action rather than on structural analysis, aroused Dewey's enduring approval.

Graduation from Vermont was followed by a brief interlude of teaching in neighboring schools. Dewey then returned to a university environment. Taking his courage in his hands (plus five hundred borrowed dollars) he enrolled in 1882 in the new and stimulating graduate school of Johns Hopkins University. In making this momentous step, he had the hearty encouragement of Professor Torrey. Here, as on other occasions in his

[1] John Dewey, "From Absolutism to Experimentalism," in *Contemporary American Philosophy*, edited by G. P. Adams and W. P. Montague (New York: The Macmillan Company, 1930), Vol. II, p. 11.

early career, he received valuable advice from Dr. W. T. Harris, editor of *The Journal of Speculative Philosophy*—an influential educator and exponent of German philosophy.

Dewey's life in Baltimore served to intensify his basic ideas and clarify their import. His associations with faculty and students were highly effective in encouraging his intellectual growth; they also issued in lifelong friendships and offers of teaching positions. Of outstanding importance was the influence of Professor George Sylvester Morris. To appreciate this, one must remember that the cultural environment of New England stressed hard and fast distinctions. For example: God was separated from the world, the mind from the body. This aroused in Dewey a profound dissatisfaction. He felt that unification is more fundamental than apparent extreme differentiation. Morris' skillful and enthusiastic advocacy of Hegel's "unifying philosophy" produced an immediate and highly appreciative reaction. Here at last was an intellectual system which satisfied both heart and head. As the years passed "salvation by Hegel" lost its appeal. However, the inspiration of the sincere and energetic personality of G. S. Morris never faded from the experience of John Dewey. This early study of Hegel "left a permanent deposit in his thinking." [2] There is, for instance, the conviction that the cultural environment shapes the beliefs of men. The enduring influence of Morris in a specific field is shown in Dewey's continuing interest in logic.

---

[2] *The Philosophy of John Dewey*, edited by P. A. Schilpp (Evanston, Ill.: Northwestern University, 1939), p. 17.

Following his graduation from Johns Hopkins, Dewey went successively to the universities of Michigan (1884), Chicago (1894), and finally Columbia (1904). The Michigan period was interrupted by one year spent at Minnesota. This teaching career at important centers of American education was extremely influential, both in the universities and their constituencies and on John Dewey. He changed from a shy scholar to a persistent, quietly dynamic applier of scientific wisdom to crucial human problems. This transition was made possible by the loyal assistance of friends too numerous to mention in this brief sketch.[3]

Few men have been more fortunate in their acquaintances and social intimates than John Dewey. There is, however, an obvious explanation—the man himself. Second to none in encouraging his development was a young lady whom he met at his first boarding house in Ann Arbor. Two years later Miss Alice Chipman became Mrs. John Dewey. Down through the years her realistic nature greatly facilitated Dewey's increasing tendency to concentrate on practical problems—the linking of theory to problems of vital human significance.

At Michigan he was a hearty exponent of educational reform. The years in Chicago gave him an opportunity to tackle such problems at close range in his experimental school. His contacts with the "underprivileged" in the Hull House area brought him face to face with social difficulties having an industrial basis. In the pulsating Midwest Dewey

---

[3] See "Biography of John Dewey" in *The Philosophy of John Dewey*, pp. 3–45.

became increasingly aware of the essential relationship of thought and action, of the fact that life is a series of problems.

The wider environment of New York extended the range of his interests without eliminating the ones already in operation. He refused to indulge in pious generalities or pained silences. He expressed specific opinions on complex contemporary problems—opinions based on a scientific approach to the actual situation. He participated very actively in several political campaigns, notably the 1912 Bull Moose campaign and the LaFollette campaign of 1924. Dewey's support for the cause of the enfranchisement of women was continuous and vigorous. His influence helped found the American Association of University Professors.

From Columbia, John Dewey went out through the world, to China, Japan, Russia, Turkey, Mexico, South Africa. In all these various projects he demonstrated, unfailingly, the power of ideals which have a natural basis in the needs of men. Everywhere he strengthened the cause of true democracy.

Few men have traveled as widely as John Dewey in order to provide personal exposition of their philosophy. One may legitimately ask whether any major thinker, in recent times, has written as many sound books and articles as "America's Philosopher."

John Dewey has been called "The Philosopher of the Common Man." This title is very appropriate. Few men have been concerned more honestly and directly with the everyday problems of ordinary people. Few thinkers have performed more effectively the philosophical functions of clarifying the nature of these problems and suggesting and illustrating the method by which they may be solved.

According to Dewey's analysis, the basic difficulty confronting contemporary men is that of achieving an effective union of thought and action, focused on the real problems which arise in the world of nature. More specifically, he notes that while we have amazing competence in dealing with inanimate nature our approach to human problems is sadly deficient. The extent and depth of this inadequacy are vigorously sketched.

He contends that we live in a culture which emphasizes the making and spending of money—to the practical exclusion of other values. Thus we miss most of the goods which really enrich life. Our development is stunted and distorted; we have little or no control over our destinies. This we clearly realize and neurotically bewail. In the world of business, large corporations "call the tune." We are able to read but don't know *what* to read. As a result we are like chips in the whirlpool of propaganda which ever swirls about us. We give frantic lip service to high ideals—truth, beauty, goodness, and the rest. Yet we stress the fact that they are very lofty and that our reach is, alas, definitely restricted. In short, we are alive; we have the means of living well; but we have not formulated sound goals. Until this is done, and adequate means developed for the achievement of these goals, we and all our kind will continue in our present sad condition.

In Dewey's opinion, tremendous improvement is well within the range of human competence. All that needs to be done is to make serious use of the methods and attitudes which have been so successful in dealing with the problems of natural science. In the past this has not been done because of mistaken theories, traditionally sanctioned, but unsupported by fact. When these absurdities are recognized and removed, the task of reconstruction can proceed.

Dewey demonstrates impressive skill in revealing the faulty assumptions which have inhibited creative human effort. He suggests that in the distant past men, unable to control their natural environment, turned to another world, the world of thought. Here there was an escape from the restrictions and failures of everyday experience. In order to justify their withdrawal from the world of nature, they claimed that thinking is more important than doing. It follows that the objects of thought are real and the practical affairs of ordinary living are unreal. This discriminative divorce of thought from action was of course supported by those members of society who, because of wealth and power, did not have to work with their hands. This socially conditioned separation of thought and action also issued in the establishment of an artificial gulf between the mind (concerned with thought) and the body (concerned with action). This point of view further contends that value ideals are eternal, passively viewed by reason, or revealed by some external authority. Individuals are expected to exemplify these ideals in their private lives. However virtue is a purely internal achievement. There is no need for social reform or a change in the techniques of social living. All these objectionable features of the traditional point of view are supplemented by the regrettable tendency to generate pseudo-problems. This results in disregarding a number of genuine ones. For instance men have been so busy trying to figure out *how* nature can be known, *how* the mind can influence the body, that they have not devoted enough time to such a real problem as how to live together with maximum value for all concerned.

One of Dewey's most fundamental convictions is that "the method we term 'scientific' [4] forms for the modern man . . . the sole dependable means for disclosing the realities of existence." [5] In his opinion there are no limits to the use of this method in dealing with the vast realm of nature. It is the means by which men can achieve control of, and security in, the entire natural environment—physical, human and cultural. This is the only foundation on which man's confidence in himself can be established firmly.

Not only is it important that scientific *method* be used in dealing with all problems; it is equally essential that

---

[4] Scientific method, according to Dewey's analysis, involves the following interrelated stages: (a) careful observation to determine the nature of the problem; (b) formation of guiding hypotheses (suggested solutions) to locate new material and in general direct subsequent operations; (c) deductions and calculations to organize available data; (d) operations to achieve an integrated situation which is a satisfactory solution to the problem, thus testing ideas involved in the hypothesis.

[5] *Living Philosophies* (New York: Simon and Schuster, 1931), p. 24.

scientific *attitudes* be manifest. The scientific attitude "on
its negative side . . . is freedom from control by routine,
prejudice, dogma, unexamined tradition, sheer self-interest.
Positively it is the will to inquire, to examine, to discriminate, to draw conclusions only on the basis of evidence after
taking pains to gather all available evidence." [6] Those
possessing this attitude regard all ideas as working hypotheses, to be tested by consequences. Such persons genuinely
enjoy all new problems and all forward-looking activities.
Thus the scientific attitude is characterized by "open-
mindedness." However it must be noted that this

> . . . is very different from empty-mindedness. While it *is* hospitality
> to new themes, facts, ideas, questions, it is not the kind of hospitality
> that would be indicated by hanging out a sign: 'Come right in; there is
> nobody at home.' It includes an active desire to listen to more sides than
> one; to give heed to facts from whatever source they come; to give full
> attention to alternative possibilities; to recognize the possibility of error
> even in the beliefs that are dearest to us.[7]

In commenting on his own philosophical activity, Dewey
emphasizes the fact that one of his main problems has been
to determine the relation of physical science to the things of
ordinary experience.[8] The preceding discussion has indicated
his devotion to the methods and attitudes employed in contemporary science. It is of fundamental importance to realize
that, while he is convinced that this is the only proper
method of obtaining knowledge, he does not give blind alle-

---

[6] *International Encyclopedia of Unified Science* (Chicago: University of Chicago
Press), Vol. I, No. 1, p. 31.

[7] *How We Think* (New York: D. C. Heath and Company, 1933 edition), p. 30.

[8] See *The Philosophy of John Dewey*, p. 523.

giance to the *data* of science. Neither does he attempt to describe or explain all experience in terms of the contents of *natural science*. Science is a tool to be used, not a deity to be worshiped.

To begin with, science is not concerned with some so-called underlying or absolute reality—some "inner nature" of things. It is interested in "those connections of things with one another that determine outcomes and hence can be used as means." [9] In order to carry out this project, modern science finds it necessary to think of natural objects in numerical terms. Thus "red" is regarded as a certain number of changes and "green" as a different number of changes (vibrations). It is ridiculous in the extreme to assume that because scientific thinking uses quantitative concepts, therefore we must disregard all other forms of experience. Persons in penitentiaries are assigned numbers. This is a convenient way of referring to them, but no one would claim that the numerical symbol is the only real aspect of the person in question. To repeat, scientific concepts are instruments used for a specific purpose:

These ways of thinking are no more rivals of or substitutes for objects as directly perceived and enjoyed than the power-loom, which is a more effective instrument for weaving cloth than was the old hand-loom, is a substitute and rival for cloth. The man who is disappointed and tragic because he cannot wear a loom is in reality no more ridiculous than are the persons who feel troubled because the objects of scientific conception of natural things have not the same uses and values as the things of direct experience.[10]

---

[9] *Experience and Nature* (New York: W. W. Norton and Company, 1929), p. v.
[10] *The Quest for Certainty* (New York: Minton, Balch and Company, 1929), p. 136.

While science is limited in the type of concept it uses, there is, in Dewey's opinion, no justification for claiming that the scientific method of reflective inquiry is confined to a restricted area. The deficiencies are found not in the method but rather in those who do not use it properly.

The clarification of these points is one of Dewey's great services to this generation. Far too many men have misunderstood the nature of scientific concepts and have felt obliged to read out of the universe all qualitative data. This involves, in particular, the exclusion of all value experience. Dewey is careful to emphasize that science does not eliminate concern for "ends." Rather, modern science is responsible for an inquiring attitude which has been fruitful in selecting new goals. Further, the techniques of science have placed at our disposal more effective means of realizing both old and new ends. Far from promoting a disregard of qualitative experience, contemporary science makes it possible to extend and enrich qualitative experience. We have heard too much of the destructive characteristics of science. It should be realized that true science is unmistakably constructive. Genuine science is destructive of *some* old beliefs and procedures, but these are consigned to the scrap heap only because they have no legitimate place in human experience. Equally important is Dewey's courageous refusal to bow meekly before the blasts of those who would confine the method of science to only one phase of human experience.

One very impressive feature of Dewey's writing is his fund of information concerning the work of previous thinkers.

He is on familiar terms with Plato, Aristotle, Bacon, Spinoza, Locke, Kant, Hegel, Lotze, Rousseau, Mill, Spencer, Bergson, James, Froebel, Pestalozzi—to mention only a few. Frequently his own point of view is presented in meticulous, detailed opposition to the system of one of the great thinkers of bygone days. On occasion a brief and brilliant comparative contrast clarifies his position. In all these references the wisdom of the past is not regarded as something to be admired in silent awe. Rather, it is material to be used in dealing with modern problems. In most cases the material must undergo rigorous reconstruction. Dewey's attitude is effectively summarized in the following passage:

> A philosopher who would relate his thinking to present civilization, in its predominantly technological and industrial character, cannot ignore any of these movements [eighteenth-century rationalism, German Idealism, the religious and philosophic traditions of Europe] any more than he can dispense with consideration of the underlying classic tradition formed in Greece and the Middle Ages. If he ignores traditions, his thoughts become thin and empty. But they are something to be employed, not just treated with respect or dressed out in a new vocabulary.[11]

A number of basic notions are inescapably involved in all phases of Dewey's thinking. In addition to the general emphasis on scientific method and scientific attitudes, there are several more specific "leading ideas." He contends that every existent is an "event." That is to say, "change" is an essential characteristic of the universe. Events (persons and things) are in constant "interaction." Dewey's refusal to

---

[11] *Whither Mankind*, edited by Charles Beard (New York: Longmans, Green, and Co., 1937), p. 330,

accept artificially isolated data is one of his chief characteristics. In this unceasing process of interaction, events do not
lose their "individuality." Each event is unique. Further,
there is a genuine "spontaneity" in the universe. "We live
in a world which is an impressive and irresistible mixture of
sufficiencies, tight completenesses, order, recurrences which
make possible prediction and control, and singularities, am-
biguities, uncertain possibilities, processes going on to consequences as yet indeterminate." [12]

Involved in this set of basic ideas are a number of very
important practical consequences. For example: (a) The
significance of each individual human being cannot be disregarded. (b) Human activities are to be understood as at-
tempts of an organism to adjust to the environment, physical, social and cultural. (c) Artificial distinctions between
ends and means, thought and action, body and mind, must
be abandoned. (d) There is one world, the world of nature.
There is no "supernatural" realm.

These and other more specific implications will be examined in the subsequent sections of this introductory essay.
In passing, it should be noted that many of these basic concepts are obviously derived from, or supported by, contemporary science. Recent developments in physics stress
"events" and "field" interaction. Heisenberg's "principle of
indeterminacy" fits in with Dewey's emphasis on spontaneity. Modern biology, of course, "underlines" interaction
and transition. The natural-science emphasis on publicly

---

[12] *Experience and Nature*, p. 47.

observable facts, and the similar approach in Behavioristic Psychology, are other important influences. However, as has been noted, Dewey is not a slavish appropriator of scientific data. He uses material only if it passes through the filter of his common sense and is verified by continuous reference to all phases of human experience.

Dewey's profound respect for scientific methods issues in his contention that genuine thinking is problem-solving. Further, it is argued that knowledge is not the mere awareness of data. The knower is not a passive spectator of the passage of events, but an active participator. Knowledge is the end result of an activity whereby a problem situation is satisfactorily settled. Thus knowing inescapably involves rationally guided doing. For example a doctor cannot know what disease a patient has until after certain activities have occurred—tapping the chest, taking the temperature, and so on. These activities of course are directed by theories derived from past experience. This newly acquired knowledge is then available to guide subsequent activities. It should be realized that while Dewey continually argues that we should concern ourselves with practical problems and avoid the pseudo-difficulties which our culture has foisted upon us, he does not use the term "practical" in any narrow sense. It is not restricted to "bread and butter" concerns. Esthetic, moral, political, religious problems are practical and require the same treatment as those problems which arise in the area of business and the familiar concerns of everyday living.

Since thinking and knowing are practical activities, involved in the adjustment of an organism to its environment, it follows that the term "mind" does not refer to a mysterious entity set apart, in lofty grandeur, from natural processes. Rather, it is the system of meanings accumulated by past knowing processes and employed by the organism when confronted by present problems. These meanings involve language—not just words, but also gestures and the various products of industrial and fine arts. Language, as a means of communication, is essential in establishing and expanding mental activity.

Dewey does not make the mistake of concentrating on only one phase of mental activity. In addition to thinking, other aspects are discussed. His treatment of the dynamic nature of habits is an important corrective of the usual overemphasis on repetition. Further, he is very critical of those who attempt to explain all human behavior in terms of a few, clear-cut, unchanging, motives—mastery, hunger, or sex. In his opinion, the basic urge of an organism is to *grow*. This is expressed in the more specific form of desire for mastery or one of the others. However, the impact of environmental conditions produces fundamental changes in the content and expression of these familiar motives. Incidentally he calls attention to the fallacy involved in popular discussions of "egoism." This arises because people confuse "acting as a self" with "acting for the self." In other words, just because there is a self acting this does not mean that the self acts only with reference to its own private interests to the exclusion of the general good.

It should be obvious from the foregoing that an individual, a person, is not something ready-made. He is the continually changing outcome of a long process of development. These changes occur, selfhood emerges, as the result of interaction with the environment. This implies that if there is to be an improvement in the self there must be a change in the environment as well as a "change of heart." Unless the "changed man" lives in a changed world, the so-called internal change is open to grave suspicion. There is a fine passage in *Experience and Nature* which states, with dynamic clarity, Dewey's convictions concerning man's place and prospects in the world:

> A mind that has opened itself to experience and that has ripened through its discipline knows its own littleness and impotencies; it knows that its wishes and acknowledgments are not final measures of the universe whether in knowledge or in conduct, and hence are, in the end, transient. But it also knows that its juvenile assumption of power and achievement is not a dream to be wholly forgotten. It implies a unity with the universe that is to be preserved. The belief, and the effort of thought and struggle which it inspires, are also the doing of the universe, and they in some way, however slight, carry the universe forward. A chastened sense of our importance, apprehension that it is not a yardstick by which to measure the whole, is consistent with the belief that we and our endeavors are significant not only for themselves but in the whole.[13]

Dewey's general position with reference to value is very effectively summarized in the following statement: "Man's

---

[13] *Experience and Nature*, p. 420.

home is nature; his purposes and aims are dependent for
execution upon natural conditions. Separated from such
conditions they become empty dreams and idle indulgences
of fancy." [14] More specifically, he claims that our value
ideals are projections of our natural urges, formulated after
careful study of their fundamental implications. Concrete
value experiences involve the satisfaction of these desires.
However, Dewey is careful to point out that everything
desired is not truly valuable. The same method of thinking
applies in dealing with value problems as in using scientific
data. "To call an object a value is to assert that it satisfies
or fulfills certain conditions." [15] This conclusion, of course,
can be reached only after a program of inquiry which con-
cludes in an examination of consequences in personal and
social experiences. These consequences are judged in terms
of the degree to which they facilitate the growth process.
Any more specific goal, set up as an absolute, does less than
justice to the complexities and rich potentialities of life.
Even reflective thinking, highly regarded as it is, is valuable
because of its function in dealing with the problems of
living. Dewey states it thus: "The dominant vocation of all
human beings at all times is living—intellectual and moral
growth." [16]

His approach to the traditional values—truth, beauty,
goodness—is entirely consistent with his general theory of
value. The truth or falsehood of judgments is conditioned,

---

[14] *Democracy and Education* (New York: The Macmillan Company, 1916), p. 333.
[15] *The Quest for Certainty*, p. 260.
[16] *Democracy and Education*, p. 362.

indeed constituted, by the consequences of its experimental application. "This event or issue of such action *is* the truth or falsity of the judgment." [17]

Dewey's discussion of moral goodness embodies his emphasis on the interaction of organism and environment and his stress on the achievement of full development. "To possess virtue does not signify to have cultivated a few namable and exclusive traits; it means to be fully and adequately what one is capable of becoming through association with others in all the offices of life." [18] Incidentally, Dewey contends that moral training can be effectively carried out in a properly directed school. His discussions of education and social philosophy include specific comments concerning personal and social morality. These will be noted in subsequent sections. In any case, it is well to realize that in all considerations of moral experience, Dewey deplores the present scandalous gulf which yawns between theory and practice. Because men have set up high ideals and disregarded "gross means," the ideals have remained unrealized. A man who holds aloft an ideal without attempting to develop the means for its achievement is manifesting either sentimental indulgence or insincerity. Ends and means must be considered together. Actions without ideals, ideals unlinked to action, are equally unsatisfactory. One without the other encourages chaos.

---

[17] *Essays in Experimental Logic* (Chicago: University of Chicago Press, 1916), p. 346.

[18] *Democracy and Education*, p. 415.

A work of art is not a picture, a statue, a poem, or a symphony. These so-called "works of art" are really "art products." This apparently subtle distinction emphasizes a very important contribution made by Dewey. A genuine work of art is an *experience*. It is an experience in which a person, in interaction with his environment, achieves a creative ordering of diverse elements in such a fashion that completeness and unity are attained. This unified experience constitutes an expansion and enrichment of life. Dewey contends that no one can have an esthetic experience when confronted by an art product unless a process of re-creation occurs—the re-creation of an experience comparable to that of the artist. Thus a musical score is not a work of art for a music lover until he plays it or experiences it in imagination. Until that occurs it is merely a symbol of a work of art. It is obvious then that art experience is inescapably linked with the environment in which it occurs, physical, economic, social, and cultural.

Dewey suggests that the distinction between esthetic experience and everyday activity is not as great as is usually assumed. Indeed he argues that in so far as an experience has singleness and coherence it possesses esthetic quality. This may be true of philosophic, scientific, industrial, and political experience. However, these are predominately practical in purpose. On the other hand, a *distinctively* esthetic experience is one in which there is no narrowly specialized concern. The purpose is enhancement of life in general. In any case it is obvious that he is attempting to "restore continuity between the refined and intensified forms of experience that are works of art and everyday events." [19] Art products have been hidden away in museums and the homes of the very rich. Genuine esthetic experience has been regarded as the privilege of the few, an unnecessary luxury for the many. Dewey believes that esthetic experience is necessary for all, since it is one of the chief means of the enrichment of life. Its fruits are serenity, a sense of the interrelations of things, and an awareness of goals beyond present achievement.

The conviction that nature is continually changing issues in a profound dissatisfaction with the type of religion which emphasizes static dogma, institutions, and procedures. The otherworldliness of traditional religion is also opposed. Another phase of his criticism of religion is clearly stated in the following:

A religion that began as a demand for a revolutionary change and that has become a sanction to establish economic, political, and international institutions should perhaps lead its sincere devotees to reflect upon the sayings of the one worshiped as its founder: "Woe unto you when all men shall speak well of you," and, "Blessed are ye when men shall revile you and persecute you." [20]

He notes that the religious stress on the individual soul has frequently led to a warped and undeveloped soul. There is no real integration of personality unless the person is a member of a co-operatively unified society. Further, many re-

---

[19] *Art as Experience* (New York: Minton, Balch and Company, 1934), p. 3.
[20] *Living Philosophies*, p. 29.

ligions have had the misfortune to identify themselves with a scientific point of view which later became outmoded. The religious claim of accuracy, if not infallibility, makes such a situation very uncomfortable for the devotees of this type of religion. When a religion sets itself up as a rival of science, in the field of science, it fights a losing battle.

Dewey suggests that the proper procedure in religion is to refrain from contentions about matters of fact—scientific or metaphysical. Attention should be concentrated on ideals to be realized in the future, not on past guarantees of present status. Religion would thus shift its attitude from that of a feeble and fearful defense to the courageous, forward striving of its founders. The ideals to be realized by this new, or reborn, type of religion would be those based on nature. There would still be a place for piety, for the sense of dependence; but it is nature, not the supernatural, which would be the focus of these attitudes. "Nature, including humanity, with all its defects and imperfections, may evoke heartfelt piety as the source of ideals, of possibilities, of aspiration in their behalf, and as the eventual abode of all attained goods and excellencies." [21]

Since these ideals are set up and used in the course of human inquiry, they cannot legitimately be given absolute and eternal status or made an excuse for haughty pride mixed with bigoted intolerance. Religions which divide men are not true religions. These ideas and techniques are tentative plans for action, to be tested in the arena of human

---

[21] *The Quest for Certainty*, p. 306.

affairs. Incidently there are unmistakable religious values in the scientific reverence for truth and in the moral aspects of democratic living.

He states that "any activity pursued in behalf of an ideal end against obstacles and in spite of threats of personal loss because of conviction of its general and enduring value is religious in quality." [22] He uses the word "God" to refer to the situation where there is a serious attempt on the part of men to use natural forces in order to achieve these high ideals. Dewey does not recommend the abandonment of religious institutions and symbols. They should be reconstructed so that they function as instruments for the expression of ideals and the re-enforcement of practical devotion to them. Thus religion may take its proper place in all the affairs of life.

Dewey's general approach to economic activities involves the demand that the "means by which we make a living be transformed into ways of making a life that is worth the living." [23] The desperate need for this transformation is repeatedly stressed. It is pointed out that many men are "hands" only. "Their hearts and brains are not engaged. They execute plans which they do not form, and of whose meaning and intent they are ignorant—beyond the fact that these plans make a profit for others and secure a wage for

---

[22] *A Common Faith* (New Haven, Conn.: Yale University Press, 1934), p. 27.
[23] *The Philosophy of John Dewey*, p. 423. This statement occurs in the excellent study contributed by Professor J. L. Childs.

themselves." [24] This restriction of activity to a narrow range produces a warping and distortion of personality which is disastrous beyond words. The intellectual and moral life of the worker suffers. Also the favored few, who exercise control, lose much of the best which life can offer. The aggressive pursuit of power and profit, to the exclusion of other values, exacts a high price in terms of lost opportunities for expansion and enrichment of life. Dewey's solution is that the processes of industry should be conducted in a co-operative fashion in the interest of genuine social utility. If the workers have an opportunity to share with managers and public officials the problems of an industry directed to the good of all, industrial life can become more meaningful and satisfactory to all concerned. He notes that the practical efficiency of this ideal scheme has been demonstrated in several previously difficult situations. This approach to economic problems must be set in its wider context of political theorizing.

There has been considerable emphasis on the rights of individuals in our political heritage. This so-called theory of "liberalism" is subjected to penetrating analysis. It is pointed out that the early form of liberalism (typified by John Locke) was used by businessmen to justify their escape from the restrictive control of the nobility. As such, this theory served a useful purpose in its day. However,

---

[24] *Individualism, Old and New* (New York: Minton, Balch and Company, 1930), p. 132.

Dewey argues that, with changing conditions, traditional liberalism (individualism) now functions as an instrument of repression used to stifle much needed social reform. The "property rights" of a few men, who own large corporations, are used to deny the conditions of satisfactory living to millions of men and women. Thus it is Dewey's strong conviction that a new, or at least revised, concept of the economic and political rights of the individual must be formulated. We must create, for today, a theory which stresses the idea that true individualism involves the participation of each in a co-operative attempt to remove the barriers which stand in the way of the enhancement of the lives of all. Specifically, the concept "liberty" should come to mean not just escape from chattel slavery, or serfdom, or dynastic rule, or restrictive traditions; rather it should imply "liberation from material insecurity and from the coercions and repressions that prevent multitudes from participation in the vast cultural resources that are at hand." [25]

In the course of his discussion of "freedom" Dewey opposes the widely accepted notion that freedom of speech is independent of freedom of thought. This is to say that though you can stop a person from talking (or writing), you cannot prevent him from thinking, since that is an internal activity. In rebuttal he argues that many thoughts are aroused through their expression by others. Further, thoughts are clarified and kept vital by communicating them to others and receiving resultant criticisms.

---

[25] *Liberalism and Social Action* (New York: G. P. Putnam's Sons, 1935), p. 48.

Dewey finds the best form of political organization in an ideal democracy. Here each individual is regarded as the possessor of worth and dignity. It follows that each individual should be encouraged to develop his own distinctive capacities in such a fashion as to contribute to the "all-around growth" not only of himself but also of all other members of society. Democracy is a way of life based on the assumption that human beings are capable of intelligent action—if proper conditions are present. The intelligent approach to a situation involving differences of opinion consists of consultation, negotiation, persuasion, rather than blind, brute force, or sly search for unfair advantage.

Of course Dewey is well aware of the deficiencies of actual democracies. As has been noted, he emphasizes the unfortunate consequences which follow from the concentration of power in a few hands. The incompetence and greed of office-holders, the apathy of those who neglect to vote or vote in ignorance, the demagoguery which disgraces election campaigns—all these and many more are sadly listed. He stresses the fact that these tendencies have within them the seeds of totalitarianism. However, and despite all this, he contends that democratic "machinery"—several conflicting parties, frequent elections, the undoubted power of aroused public opinion—seems likely to provide effective correctives.

It is important to observe that while Dewey does assign very great efficacy to economic forces he absolutely refuses to accept the Marxian philosophy of history. The assumed inevitability of the dialectical process and the emphasis on violence are repugnant to him. He points out that there is no place for dogmatic certainty if one follows the lead of modern science. The much-vaunted scientific approach of Marx is the outmoded science of the nineteenth century, which stressed inevitable sequence in accordance with all-encompassing law. In the modern world, laws are statistical generalities, probable only. These are laws which have not been brought into a unified system. In any case there is no real place in the Marxist theory for the creative work of human intellectual inquiry.

Dewey's general approach to political problems is clearly indicated in these comments:

> In the world of natural change, men learned control by means of the systematic invention of effective tools only when they gave up preoccupation with lofty principles logically arranged, and occupied themselves seriously with the turmoil of concrete observable changes. Till we accomplish a like revolution in social and moral affairs, our politics will continue to be an idle spectator of an alternation of social comedies and tragedies, compensating for its impotency by reducing its applause and hisses to a scheme of fixed canons which the show is then imagined to exemplify.[26]

Dewey's discussion of education concentrates attention on the development of young children. Thus he states that the purpose of education is "to give the young the things they need in order to develop in an orderly, sequential way into members of society." [27] Contrary to many educators, he stresses the fact that several aspects of the child's personality

---

[26] *Character and Events* (New York: Henry Holt and Company, 1929), p. 732.
[27] *Education Today* (New York: G. P. Putnam's Sons, 1940), p. 269.

require attention. In addition to the intellectual segment of
the total personality, there are the physical, social, and value
phases of experience. Thus the school should attempt to
develop not only competence in managing resources and
overcoming obstacles human and inanimate, but also, more
specifically, sociability, esthetic taste, sound intellectual
methods, and sensitiveness to the rights and claims of
others. These goals of education constitute the criteria of
an adequate education. Thus it is obvious that in Dewey's
opinion education should be—and should prepare for—truly
democratic living.

If education is to perform this function, it must involve
active community life within the school and a genuine and
vital interaction with available material resources and the
social environment. More specifically, it must be remem-
bered that the school is only one of many agencies of education. In many instances it is only a minor force.

A child should be encouraged to study what interests him
and in a fashion which seems natural. This rules out the
common pedagogical procedure of attempting to arouse interest in a subject matter by artificially linking it with
pleasurable experiences. As a matter of fact, this technique
is entirely unnecessary. There are plenty of educative materials which naturally arouse the interest of a child. For example, a lesson in history can develop from the observation
of some near-by historic monument. Geography may be ap-
proached by means of a trip to a lake or river. Physics and
chemistry can be introduced in the process of preparing a

school lunch. Social institutions may be examined in the course of a tour of the community.

Underlying all Dewey's educational philosophy is the conviction that an individual is both "body" and "mind." The development and well-being of both must be considered constantly, by any effective educator. By reference to actual situations, rural and urban, Dewey shows, in considerable detail, how his method can be applied within the general framework of our present educational system.[28] In the course of emphasizing the importance of bodily, as well as mental, development, Dewey recommends "shop work." However, it is to be noted that the value of shop work lies not only in the fact that it is in accordance with the child's desire to make things, or that it provides the basis of vocational skills which later may have a bread-and-butter value. These of course are of importance. Yet of far greater worth are social skills, the ability to solve co-operatively problems which arise in this context. Here also students develop personal initiative. Dewey deplores the tendency to restrict cultural education to a few upper-class people while providing only shop skills for potential workers. If the workers are to be capable of valid value judgments, they must have a liberal education as well as mechanical training. This does not mean the reproduction of some archaic sophistication. Rather Dewey is advocating a comprehensive and enlightened approach to the problems of the modern world. In other words,

---

[28] See, for example, *Schools of Tomorrow* (New York: E. P. Dutton and Company, 1915).

culture is synonymous with social efficiency. By the same token, those who are not likely to have to work with their hands will derive value from shop work because of the bodily skills and socializing experience which it gives.

Dewey calls attention to the fact that the drill method of teaching kills initiative. It is far wiser, for example, to encourage a child to learn arithmetic when it is relevant to the solving of some problem such as the building of a model bridge. Reading will be undertaken naturally when a child wants to obtain more information about some project in which he is engaged. Writing will obviously be required as a tool useful in recording and sharing results.

In this new type of educational procedure, the teacher is tremendously important, indeed more important than in the traditional system. This is so because it is more difficult to direct natural activities along a coherent line of development than to follow a previously fixed programme. "The educator's part in the enterprise of education is to furnish the environment which stimulates responses and directs the learner's course." [29] It should be clear that Dewey does not advocate the undirected expression of childish whim and immature desire. True, the teacher "drives with a light rein"; but he still exercises control. It is a case of advice presented in such a fashion that its value is appreciated by the student rather than "do this because I say so." This technique of course involves a new approach to the problem of discipline. The ideal situation is that in which the child,

---

[29] *Democracy and Education*, p. 212.

having profited from educational experience, has developed intelligent habits of living. True discipline is not externally imposed.

The traditional notion that education is essentially preparation for the future has tended to distract attention from pressing present problems. This extreme futuristic stress overlooks the fact that children are chiefly interested in the present. Even those who try to make a detailed present approach to specific future problems are frequently involved in difficulties. The process of change is so rapid these days that it is very difficult to predict what the future will be like. Frequently skills are taught which were effective a few years ago but are now going out of fashion and will be definitely antiquated a few years hence. In Dewey's opinion the best training for the future is in general methods and attitudes which will enable a person to adjust himself to changing conditions with confidence and efficiency.

The need for these various educational reforms is crucial. Traditional education has been undermining our democratic way of life. The political implications of our present educational system must be faced in a realistic fashion. An obnoxious class distinction, based on the gulf between cultural and technical education, has been set up. It is widely assumed that the great majority of our people should be trained to be efficient "industrial fodder," not as citizens genuinely participating in the affairs of society. The organization of many schools is such that initiative and concern for others are stifled both in students and in teachers.

Ruthless competition rather than genuine co-operation is the rule rather than the exception. Natural interest and pleasure seldom accompany the activities of traditional education; fear is the predominant motive. This state of affairs is found not only in most elementary and high schools; it is prevalent also on the college level. This, re-marks Dewey, is merely a reflection of the total culture, of which our educational system is a part. In so far as this is so, the spirit of democracy is sadly lacking. It is Dewey's conviction that "education is the fundamental method of social progress and reform." [30] Thus it follows that if our democratic society is to be strengthened against its many enemies, the school must play its part, not only in word but also in deed.

Dewey's literary style is characterized, on occasion, by the skillful use of vividly ironic analogies which considerably clarify his point of view. For example, he suggests that those who try to extend knowledge by linking sensations together (rather than using them as starting points in a process of inquiry) are like a man who assumes that you can get rid of the irritation caused by a grain of sand in the eye by substituting a pile of sand. He remarks that those who con-centrate on ends and disregard means are like a man who claims that he wants to paint a picture but who has no interest in canvas, brush, and paints. He pokes fun at solemn pseudo-problems such as that of the body-mind relationship.

[30] *Education Today*, p. 15.

It is just as mysterious that body and mind should be related as that a plant should grow in the soil. Theories are tested as glasses are tested. The criterion is: Do things assume a more orderly and clear aspect? The attempt to understand something in isolation from its context is like trying to understand a loom without any reference to the yarn which it spins into cloth.[31]

It is interesting to note that despite Dewey's strong negative reaction to traditional religion, a certain amount of Biblical phraseology crops up in his writing. There is, for example, the passage reminiscent of the Bible's "Consider the lilies of the field, how they grow; they toil not, neither do they spin." Dewey says: "Consider the utilitarians how they toiled, spun, and wove, but who never saw man arrayed in joy as the lilies of the field." [32] In the course of a discussion of the practical implications of inference he refers to Noah and his ark.[33] The Biblical query "What will it profit a man if he gain the whole world and lose his own soul" is probably the basis of Dewey's question "What will it profit a man to do this, that, and the other specific thing, if he has no clear idea of why he is doing them?" [34] The observation that "We reap where we have not sown" is used on several occasions.[35]

---

[31] See *The Quest for Certainty*, pp. 113, 279; *Experience and Nature*, p. 277; *Essays in Experimental Logic*, p. 198; *Philosophy and Civilization* (New York: Minton, Balch and Company, 1931), p. 312.

[32] *Experience and Nature*, p. 78.

[33] *Essays in Experimental Logic*, p. 423.

[34] *Education Today*, p. 302.

[35] See *Character and Events*, p. 821.

The many phases of Dewey's philosophy are all part of a
lifelong project—the attempt to formulate and apply a
philosophy of experience framed in the light of science and
modern industrial techniques,[36] a philosophy in which
"science and the arts are brought unitedly to bear upon
industry, politics, religion, domestic life, and human relations in general." [37] The end in view is the enrichment of
human life—the achievement of the maximum possible
growth in all phases of co-operative human enterprise.

Dewey's *Essays in Experimental Logic* express an appreciative evaluation of the work of William James. Because
this effective comment is strikingly relevant to Dewey's own
contributions to philosophy, it is presented herewith; the
only changes are the substitution of "instrumentalism" for
"pragmatism," and "Dewey" for "James":

> Even those who dislike instrumentalism can hardly fail to find much
> of profit in the exhibition of Dewey's instinct for concrete facts, the
> breadth of his sympathies, and his illuminating insights. Unreserved
> frankness, lucid imagination, varied contacts with life digested into sum-
> mary and trenchant conclusions, keen perceptions of human nature in
> the concrete, a constant sense of the subordination of philosophy to life,
> capacity to put things into an English which projects ideas as if bodily
> into space till they are solid things to walk around and survey from
> different sides—these things are not so common in philosophy that they
> may not smell sweet even by the name of instrumentalism.[38]

---

[36] Dewey is not unaware of the defects of modern industrial techniques and the
subtle danger of being busy for the sake of business. Thus he refers to "those modes
of mechanical distraction which are unaccountably termed efficiency" (*Education
Today*, p. 193).

[37] *Living Philosophies*, p. 34.

[38] *Essays in Experimental Logic*, p. 329.

John Dewey's books are a striking mixture of brilliant epigrams, stimulating insights, penetrating irony, and vast areas of plodding analysis. The same features, particularily the latter, characterize his lectures. For example, during the second decade of this century, at a time when he was already fully recognized as an important factor in the cultural environment, he refused to stoop to crowd-pleasing tricks. Devotees of the "latest thing in wisdom" were not impressed by the solemn man who looked like a farmer and spoke with a monotonous and husky Vermont drawl. Even bright young graduate students were amazed and disappointed. Surely this great professor should flaunt fresh lectures notes rather than those venerable yellow fragments! Incidentally, why didn't he look at his audience rather than peer abstractedly out the window? However, in the mind of the serious student these thoughts were quickly replaced by an attitude of profound respect and rapidly increasing interest. Here was a man actually thinking, encouraging others to think, avoiding none of the difficulties involved in a problem. This lack of the usual "lecture techniques" was merely a symptom of concentration on more important matters. It was also, by implication, a compliment to at least some members of the audience.

This is not to say that the occasional brilliance of his writing does not appear in the spoken word. The epigrams and ironic wit are unmistakably there. With customary insight, he once remarked that the real test of the morals of a group lies in what is regarded as evil, saying: "I think sometimes one can tell more about the morals of our society from the inmates of its jails than from the inmates of its universities." [39] With a "tongue in cheek" mixture of pride and remorse, Dewey has been heard to admit: "My ancestry is free from all blemish. All my forefathers earned an honest living as farmers, wheelwrights and coopers. I was absolutely the first one in seven generations to fall from grace." [40] These humorous asides transform his somewhat solemn visage. His face lights up. There is a grin accompanied by a diffident, dry little chuckle.

The passage of time has not removed John Dewey's evident manifestations of abundant energy. He shifts about in his chair, wiggles his toes, pulls at his mustache, or musses his white hair. Quaint phrases pop out on occasion: for instance, "sounds like" or "fork in the road." The machinery of the New England town meeting is still very much in his mind.

Like many professors, he has accumulated a reputation for absent-mindedness. At the celebration of the fiftieth anniversary of the University of Wisconsin, he received an honorary degree and promptly lost the hood. No one was at all surprised. However, his absent-mindedness is of the commendable variety. It indicates concentration on essentials. In any case the external habiliments of academic glory have never had much appeal for John Dewey. Some of his other personal traits—the apparent shyness and addiction to an-

---

[39] Irwin Edman, *Philosopher's Holiday* (New York: The Viking Press, 1938), pp. 141–42.

[40] *Time*, June 24, 1946, p. 34.

tique phrases—should be understood as charming trivia left undisturbed (because of more pressing matters) by one of the most efficient social individuals of our time.

Absence of pretentiousness, and tremendous depth and power of mind, are essential characteristics of John Dewey. The simplicity and courtesy of the truly great are striking features of his personality. He is one of those rare souls who discover more of value in most people than they find in themselves. By expecting more than the usual performance, he stimulates others to higher levels of achievement. Above all, Dewey believes that every man should have a genuine chance to develop all his powers to the full, co-operating in the common cause of enriching human life. This ideal has been translated into action on numerous occasions. Jane Addams of Hull House, caught in a cross fire between capitalists and unionists, found Professor John Dewey in the midst of the conflict actively assisting in bringing the problem to a satisfactory solution. He gave unstintingly of time and effort to secure what he thought was justice for Sacco and Vanzetti. He investigated Trotsky's claim that he had been falsely accused by Stalin and unfairly treated by the United States. These arduous tasks were undertaken not because he agrees with the social philosophy of the men concerned but rather because he felt that they should have an opportunity to state their case.

These are only a few of the striking and well-known instances of a type of activity in which he frequently engages. Indeed, many people recall that in some hour of desperate need, they found a doughty champion in John Dewey. His respect for other men (even those worthless in the eyes of the world), his humility with reference to his own abilities— these are not idle poses. However, it must be clearly realized that this mildness of manner, this sensitiveness to the feelings of others, are not sentimental softness. When Dewey considers it necessary to "hit hard" in an argument, he does so with relentless power. This man is the product of realistic, reserved, rural Vermont. He has lived in the energetic, problem-solving Midwest. For years he has been at home in the keen cosmopolitan culture of New York and the wide world which impinges upon it. An awareness of this helps us to understand the vast range of his thinking, his amazing fusion of thought and action, his unceasing devotion to causes deemed worthy of support.

The intellectual vigor of John Dewey has its basis in an impressive physical "power plant." Few men in their eighties can rise at 7:30 and hustle through a busy day of reading, writing, social activities, meetings, rummaging through book stores, interviewing public officials on behalf of a friend. But John Dewey is an unusual person. Incidentally he is not adverse to using gadgets. Of course he is committed to the theory that one should gratefully accept the practical applications of science. His electric razor is almost as important as his carpet slippers.

It becomes quickly obvious that his book-lined study is not exclusively devoted to the retention of scholarly tomes. He once amazed a representative of the press by emerging from a copy of *Too Lively To Live*—a murder mystery. This is not to say that he has neglected to keep abreast of scholarly advances. As a matter of fact, he is more "productive" than many men half his age.

John Dewey's impressive sequence of birthdays provides welcome opportunities for his friends and well-wishers to attest the extent of his influence and their appreciative devotion. Not only in education does this man loom like a colossus. In logic, esthetics, ethics, philosophy of science, religion, history of culture, his stature is only slightly less immense. Here is a true friend, a humane scholar, an efficient solver of crucial problems, a decisive factor in our civilization. John Dewey poses a tremendous problem. It is the problem of fully appreciating this, one of the finest exemplifications of our way of life. Real appreciation involves more than admiration. There is also the call to intelligent action.

The Wit and Wisdom of
John Dewey

KEY TO ABBREVIATIONS

A.E.   *Art as Experience.* New York: Minton, Balch & Co., 1934.

C.E.   *Character and Events.* New York: Henry Holt & Co., 1929.

C.F.   *A Common Faith.* New Haven: Yale University Press, 1934.

D.E.   *Democracy and Education.* New York: The Macmillan Co., 1916.

E.   *Ethics* (with J. H. Tufts). New York: Henry Holt & Co., 1932 (Revised)

E.E.   *Educational Essays.* London: Blackie & Son, 1910.

E.L.   *Essays in Experimental Logic.* Chicago: The University of Chicago Press, 1916.

E.N.   *Experience and Nature.* New York: W. W. Norton & Co., 1929.

E.T.   *Education Today.* New York: G. P. Putnam's Sons, 1940.

F.C.   *Freedom and Culture.* New York: G. P. Putnam's Sons, 1939.

G. P.   *German Philosophy and Politics.* New York: Henry Holt & Co., 1915.

H.N.C.   *Human Nature and Conduct.* New York: Henry Holt & Co., 1922.

H.W.T.   *How We Think.* New York: D. C. Heath & Co., 1933 edition.

I.M.W.   *Intelligence in the Modern World.* New York: Random House (Modern Library), 1939.

I.D.   *The Influence of Darwin on Philosophy.* New York: Henry Holt & Co., 1910.

I.O.   *Individualism Old and New.* New York: Minton, Balch & Co., 1930.

L.   *Logic: The Theory of Inquiry.* New York: Henry Holt & Co., 1938.

L.S.A.   *Liberalism nad Social Action.* New York: G. P. Putnam's Sons, 1935.

P.C.   *Philosophy and Civilization.* New York: Minton, Balch & Co., 1931.

P.D.   *The Philosophy of John Dewey.* New York: Henry Holt & Co., 1928.

P.M.   *Problems of Men.* New York: The Philosophical Library, 1946.

P.P.   *The Public and Its Problems.* New York: Henry Holt & Co., 1927.

Q.C.   *The Quest for Certainty*. New York: Minton, Balch & Co., 1929.
R.P.   *Reconstruction in Philosophy*. Boston: The Beacon Press, 1948
          (Enlarged).
S.S.E.   *The Sources of a Science of Education*. New York: H. Liveright,
          1929.
S.S.   *The School and Society*. Chicago: The University of Chicago
          Press, 1900.
S.T.   *Schools of Tomorrow*. New York: E. P. Dutton & Co., 1915.

Philosophy and Philosophers

What makes philosophy hard work, and also makes its cultivation worth while, is precisely the fact that it assumes the responsibility for setting forth some ideal of a collective good life by the methods which the best science of the day employs in its quite different task, and with the use of the characteristic knowledge of its day.   [C.E. 847]

Philosophic theory has no Aladdin's lamp to summon into immediate existence the values which it intellectually constructs. . . . Education is the laboratory in which philosophic distinctions become concrete and are tested.   [D.E. 384]

As the philosopher has received his problem from the world of action, so he must return his account there for auditing and liquidation.   [I.D. 274]

Better it is for philosophy to err in active participation in the living struggles and issues of its own age and times than to maintain an immune monastic impeccability, without relevancy and bearing in the generating ideas of its contemporary present. In the one case, it will be respected, as we respect all virtue that attests its sincerity by sharing in the perplexities and failures, as well as in the joys and triumphs, of endeavor. In the other case, it bids fair to share the fate of whatever preserves its gentility but not its activity, . . . snugly ensconced in the consciousness of its own respectability.   [P.D. 552]

The moment philosophy supposes it can find a final and comprehensive solution, it ceases to be inquiry and becomes either apologetics or progaganda.   [L. 35]

If it is better to travel than to arrive, it is because traveling is a constant arriving, while arrival that precludes further traveling is most easily attained by going to sleep or dying.   [H.N.C. 282]

Any philosophy that in its quest for certainty ignores the reality of the uncertain in the ongoing processes of nature denies the conditions out of which it arises.

[Q.C. 244]

It is an old story that philosophers, in common with theologians and social theorists, are as sure that personal habits and interests shape their opponents' doctrines as they are that their own beliefs are "absolutely" universal and objective in quality.   [E.L. 326]

Very much of what has been presented as philosophic reflection is in effect simply an idealization, for the sake of emotional satisfaction, of the brutely given state of affairs.   [G.P. 7]

There is a special service which the study of philosophy may render. Empirically pursued it will not be a study of philosophy but a study, by means of philosophy, of life-experience.   [E.N. 37]

If there are genuine uncertainties in life, philosophies must reflect that uncertainty. If there are different diagnoses of the cause of a difficulty, and different proposals for dealing with it . . . there must be divergent competing philosophies.   [D.E. 382]

Philosophers are parts of history, caught in its movement; creators perhaps in some measure of its future, but also assuredly creatures of its past.   [P.D. 453]

Classic philosophy was conceived in wonder, born in leisure, and bred in consummatory contemplation. [E.N. 123]

The Greeks employed thinking not as a means of changing given objects of observation so as to get at the conditions and effects of their occurrence, but to impose upon them certain static properties not found in them in their changeable occurrence. The essence of the static properties conferred upon them was harmony of form and pattern.   [Q.C. 90–91]

The utmost to be said in praise of Plato and Aristotle is not that they invented excellent moral theories, but that they rose to the opportunity which the spectacle of Greek life afforded.   [I.D. 46]

Metaphysics is a substitute for custom as the source and guarantor of higher moral and social values— that is the leading theme of the classic philosophy of Europe, as evolved by Plato and Aristotle.   [R. P.17]

These eternal objects abstracted from the course of events, although labeled Reality, in opposition to Appearance, are in truth but the idlest and most evanescent of appearances born of personal craving and shaped by private fantasy.   [E.N. 436]

The forms or Ideas which Plato thought were models and patterns of existing things actually had their source in Greek art, so that his treatment of artists is a supreme instance of intellectual ingratitude.   [A.E. 294]

Aristotle . . . yielded to the besetting sin of all philosophers, the idealization of the existent.   [I.D. 50]

The very fitness of the Aristotelian logical organon in respect to the culture and common sense of a certain group in the period in which it was formulated unfits it to be a logical formulation of not only the science but even of the common sense of the present cultural epoch.   [L. 65]

Aristotle doubted no more than Plato that the fully realized reality, the divine and ultimate, is changeless. Though it is called Activity or Energy, the Activity knew no change, the energy did nothing. It was the activity of an army forever marking time and never going anywhere.
[R.P. 107]

Sir Isaac Newton threw the mantle of deism about the physical universe.   [C.E. 721]

When the isolated and simple existences of Locke and Hume are seen not to be truly empirical at all but to answer to certain demands of their theory of mind, the necessity ceases for the elaborate Kantian and Post-Kantian machinery of *a priori* concepts and categories to synthesize the alleged stuff of experience.   [R.P. 90–91]

Certainly unction seems to have descended upon epistemology, in apostolic succession, from classic idealism; so that neo-Kantianism is rarely without a tone of edification, as if feeling itself the patron of man's spiritual interests in contrast to the supposed crudeness and insensitiveness of naturalism and empiricism.   [I.D. 201]

If the kingdoms of science and of righteousness nowhere touch, there can be no strife between them. Indeed, Kant sought to arrange their relations or lack of relations in such a way that there should be not merely noninterference but a pact of at least benevolent neutrality.

[Q.C. 58]

The "is" of knowledge is to be derived from the "ought to be" of morals. The effort does not seem promising; it appears to speak more for the ethical ardor of his [Kant's] [1] personality than for the sobriety of his understanding.   [Q.C. 62]

---

[1] This, and similar subsequent material in square brackets, does not occur in the text.

The alleged revolution of Kant consisted in making explicit what was implicit in the classic tradition.

[Q.C. 287]

There are thinkers full of ancestral piety, and there are thinkers who to themselves at least seem to care nothing for the past, in their eagerness to make a fresh start. It was the fate of Kant, whether fortunately or tragically, to unite the two dispositions in himself.

[C.E. 63]

Forswearing the reality of affection, and the gallantry of adventure, the genuineness of the incomplete, the tentative, it [Absolute Idealism] has taken an oath of allegiance to Reality, objective, universal, complete. . . . making a desert and calling it harmony, unity, totality.

[I.D. 172–73]

Idealistic philosophies have not been wrong in attaching vast importance and power to ideas. But in isolating their function and their test from action, they failed to grasp the point and place where ideas have a constructive office.   [Q.C. 138]

Idealism in proving that the ideal is once for all the real has absolved itself from the office, more useful if humbler, of attempting that interpretation of the actual by means of which values could be made more extensive and more secure.   [Q.C. 310]

The Absolute Experience, . . . although absolute, eternal, all-comprehensive, and pervasively integrated into a whole so logically perfect that no separate patterns, to say nothing of seams and holes, can exist in it, . . . proceeds to play a tragic joke upon itself—for there is nothing else to be fooled—by appearing in a queer combination of rags and glittering gee-gaws, in the garb of the temporal, partial, and conflicting things, mental as well as physical, of ordinary experience.   [E.N. 61]

Much of what philosophies have taught about the ideal and noumenal or superiorly real world is, after all, only casting a dream into an elaborate dialectic form through the use of a speciously scientific terminology.
[R.P. 119]

Consider the utilitarians how they toiled, spun, and wove, but who never saw man arrayed in joy as the lilies of the field. Happiness was to them a matter of calculation and effort, of industry guided by mathematical bookkeeping. The history of man shows however that man takes his enjoyment neat, and at as short range as possible.
[E.N. 78]

Utilitarianism . . . was a part of a philanthropic and reform movement of the nineteenth century. . . . It was concerned not with extracting the honey of the passing moment but with breeding improved bees and constructing hives.   [H.N.C. 205]

With Bergson, change is the creative operation of God, or *is* God—one is not quite sure which. The change of change is not only cosmic pyrotechnics, but is a process of divine, spiritual, energy. We are here in the presence of prescription, not description.   [E.N. 51]

The suggestion that pragmatism is the intellectual equivalent of commercialism need not, however, be taken too seriously. It is of that order of interpretation which would say that English neo-realism is a reflection of the aristocratic snobbery of the English; the tendency of French thought to dualism an expression of an alleged Gallic disposition to keep a mistress in addition to a wife; and the idealism of Germany a manifestation of an ability to elevate beer and sausage into a higher synthesis with the spiritual values of Beethoven and Wagner.   [C.E. 543]

I . . . affirm that the term "pragmatic" means only the rule of referring all thinking, all reflective considerations, to *consequences* for final meaning and test. Nothing is said about the nature of the consequences; they may be esthetic, or moral, or political, or religious in quality—anything you please.   [E.L. 330]

Everybody knows that the trend of modern philosophy has been to arrive at theories regarding the nature of the universe by means of theories regarding the nature of knowledge—a procedure which reverses the apparently more judicious method of the ancients in basing their conclusions about knowledge on the nature of the universe in which knowledge occurs.   [Q.C. 41]

The problem of how a mind can know an external world, or even know that there is such a thing, is like the problem of how an animal eats things external to itself; it is the kind of problem that arises only if one assumes that a hibernating bear living off its own stored substance defines the normal procedure, ignoring moreover the question where the bear got its stored material.   [E.N. 278]

In ultimate analysis the mystery that mind should use a body, or that a body should have a mind, is like the mystery that a man cultivating plants should use the soil; or that the soil which grows plants at all should grow those adapted to its own physico-chemical properties and relations.   [E.N. 277]

After all, the optimism that says that the world is already the best possible of all worlds might be regarded as the most cynical of pessimisms. If this is the best possible, what would a world which was fundamentally bad be like?   [R.P. 178]

"Common-sense" philosophy usually repeats current conventionalities. What is averred to be implicit reliance upon what is given in common experience is likely to be merely an appeal to prejudice to gain support for some fanaticism or defense for some relic of conservative tradition which is beginning to be questioned.   [E.N. 33]

Nature as it exists at any particular time is a challenge, rather than a completion; it provides possible starting points and opportunities rather than final ends.
[Q.C. 100]

We . . . find that one of the chief offices of the idea of nature in political and judicial practice has been to consecrate the existent state of affairs, whatever its distribution of advantages and disadvantages, of benefits and losses; and to idealize, rationalize, moralize, the physically given.   [C.E. 795]

When philosophy shall have co-operated with the course of events and made clear and coherent the meaning of the daily detail, science and emotion will interpenetrate, practice and imagination will embrace. Poetry and religious feeling will be the unforced flowers of life. To further this articulation and revelation of the meanings of the current course of events is the task and problem of philosophy in days of transition. [R.P. 212–13]

Thinking

To fill our heads, like a scrapbook, with this and that item as a finished and done-for thing, is not to think. It is to turn ourselves into a piece of registering apparatus. To consider the *bearing* of the occurrence upon what may be, but is not yet, is to think.　[D.E. 172]

Information severed from thoughtful action is dead, a mind-crushing load. Since it simulates knowledge and thereby develops the poison of conceit, it is a most powerful obstacle to further growth in the grace of intelligence.　[D.E. 179]

Man's home is nature; his purposes and aims are dependent for execution upon natural conditions. Separated from such conditions they become empty dreams and idle indulgences of fancy.　[D.E. 333]

The true purity of knowledge exists not when it is uncontaminated by contact with use and service. It is wholly a moral matter, an affair of honesty, impartiality and generous breadth of intent in search and communication.

[P.P. 175]

The appropriate subject matter of awareness is not reality at large, a metaphysical heaven to be mimeographed at many removes upon a badly constructed mental carbon paper which yields at best only fragmentary, blurred, and erroneous copies. Its proper and legitimate object is that relationship of organism and environment in which functioning is most amply and effectively attained.

[P.C. 48]

The need of thinking to accomplish something beyond thinking is more potent than thinking for its own sake. [H.W.T. 49]

To praise thinking above action because there is so much ill-considered action in the world is to help maintain the kind of world in which action occurs for narrow and transient purposes. To seek after ideas and to cling to them as means of conducting operations, as factors in practical arts, is to participate in creating a world in which the springs of thinking will be clear and ever-flowing.

[Q.C. 138]

Mind is no longer a spectator beholding the world from without and finding its highest satisfaction in the joy of self-sufficing contemplation. The mind is within the world as a part of the latter's own ongoing process.

[Q.C. 291]

The spectator view of knowledge, is a purely compensatory doctrine which men of an intellectual turn have built up to console themselves for the actual and social impotency of the calling of thought to which they are denoted.   [R.P. 117]

To idealize and rationalize the universe at large is after all a confession of inability to master the courses of things that specifically concern us.   [I.D. 17]

"Safety first" has played a large role in effecting a preference for knowing over doing and making. With those to whom the process of pure thinking is congenial and who have the leisure and the aptitude to pursue their preference, the happiness attending knowing is unalloyed; it is not entangled in the risks which overt action cannot escape.   [Q.C. 7]

All serious thinking combines in some proportion and perspective the actual and the possible, where actuality supplies contact and solidity while possibility furnishes the ideal upon which criticism rests and from which creative effort springs.   [C.E. 437]

There is but one sure road of access to truth —the road of patient, co-operative inquiry operating by means of observation, experiment, record, and controlled reflection.   [C.F. 32]

Experimental method is not just messing around nor doing a little of this and a little of that in the hope that things will improve. Just as in the physical sciences, it implies a coherent body of ideas, a theory, that gives direction to effort. [P.M. 137–8]

"Thought" is not a property of something termed intellect or reason apart from nature. It is a mode of directed overt action. Ideas are anticipatory plans and designs which take effect in concrete *re*constructions of antecedent conditions of existence. [Q.C. 166–67]

Failure to encourage fertility and flexibility in formation of hypotheses as frames of reference is closer to a death warrant of a science than any other one thing.

[L. 508]

Hypotheses are fruitful when they are suggested by actual need, are bulwarked by knowledge already attained, and are tested by the consequences of the operations they evoke. . . . Otherwise imagination is dissipated into fantasies and rises vaporously into the clouds.

[Q.C. 310–11]

Any belief as such is tentative, hypothetical; it is not just to be acted upon, but is to be *framed* with reference to its office as a guide to action. Consequently, it should be the last thing in the world to be picked up casually and then clung to rigidly. [Q.C. 277]

Skepticism that is not . . . a search is as much a personal emotional indulgence as is dogmatism.

[Q.C. 228]

It is notorious that a hypothesis does not have to be true in order to be highly serviceable in the conduct of inquiry.   [L. 142]

It does not pay to tether one's thoughts to the post of use with too short a rope. Power in action requires largeness of vision, which can be had only through the use of imagination.   [H.W.T. 224]

The natural man is impatient with doubt and suspense: he impatiently hurries to be shut of it. A disciplined mind takes delight in the problematic, and cherishes it until a way out is found that approves itself upon examination.   [Q.C. 228]

The office of intelligence in every problem that either a person or a community meets is to effect a working connection between old habits, customs, institutions, beliefs, and new conditions.   [L.S.A. 50]

The old and the new have forever to be integrated with each other, so that the values of old experience may become the servants and instruments of new desires and aims.   [L.S.A. 49]

The conclusions of prior knowledge are the *instruments* of new inquiries, not the norm which determines their validity.   [Q.C. 186]

Taking what is already known or pointing to it is no more a case of knowledge than taking a chisel out of a toolbox is the making of the tool.   [Q.C. 188]

The live creature adopts its past; it can make friends with even its stupidities, using them as warnings that increase present wariness. Instead of trying to live upon whatever may have been achieved in the past, it uses past successes to inform the present.   [A.E. 18]

Inference is the advance into the unknown, the use of the established to win new worlds from the void.
[E.L. 215]

The beginning of culture would be to cease plaintive eulogies of a past culture, eulogies which carry only a few yards before they are drowned in the noise of the day, and essay an imaginative insight into the possibilities of what is going on so assuredly although so blindly and crudely.   [C.E. 499]

Of course there has been an enormous increase in the amount of knowledge possessed by mankind, but it does not equal, probably, the increase in the amount of errors and half-truths which have got into circulation. [P.P. 162]

But socially as well as scientifically the great thing is not to avoid mistakes but to have them take place under conditions such that they can be utilized to increase intelligence in the future. [R.P. 208]

A great advantage of possession of the habit of reflective activity is that failure is not *mere* failure. It is instructive. The person who really thinks learns quite as much from his failures as from his successes. [H.W.T. 114]

The open mind is a nuisance if it is merely passively open to allow anything to find its way into a vacuous mind behind the opening. It is significant only as it is the mark of an actively searching mind, one on the alert for further knowledge and understanding. [I.M.W. 689–90]

Genuine ignorance is . . . profitable because it is likely to be accompanied by humility, curiosity, and open-mindedness; whereas ability to repeat catch-phrases, cant terms, familiar propositions, gives the conceit of learning and coats the mind with a varnish waterproof to new ideas. [H.W.T. 237]

 M an is not logical and his intellectual history is a record of mental reserves and compromises. He hangs on to what he can in his old beliefs even when he is compelled to surrender their logical basis.   [H.N.C. 224]

 N either the existence nor the positive value of the irrational in man is to be glossed over. All the instincts, impulses, and emotions which push man into action outside the treadmill of use and wont are irrational. The depths, the mysteries, of nature are non-rational. The business of reason is not to extinguish the fires which keep the cauldron of vitality seething, nor yet to supply the ingredients which are in vital stir. Its task is to see that they boil to some purpose.   [C.E. 587]

 I ntelligence . . . is inherently involved in action. Moreover, there is no opposition between it and emotion. There is such a thing as passionate intelligence, as ardor in behalf of light shining into the murky places of social existence, and as zeal for its refreshing and purifying effect.
[C.F. 79]

 O ur affections, when they are enlightened by understanding, are organs by which we enter into the meaning of the natural world as genuinely as by knowing, and with greater fullness and intimacy.   [Q.C. 297]

The interpretations which are embodied in the words that have come down to us are the products of desire and hope, of chance circumstance and ignorance, of the authority exercised by medicine men and priests as well as of acute observation and sound judgment.   [I.M.W. 817]

A word means one thing in relation to a religious institution, still another thing in business, a third thing in law, and so on. This fact is the real Babel of communication.   [L. 50]

Language comes infinitely short of paralleling the variegated surface of nature. Yet words as practical devices are the agencies by which the ineffable diversity of natural existence as it operates in human experience is reduced to orders, ranks, and classes that can be managed.

[A.E. 215]

Words are particularly subject to . . . [a] tendency towards automatism. If their almost mechanical sequence is not too prosaic, a writer gets the reputation of being clear merely because the meanings he expresses are so familiar as not to demand thought by the reader.

[A.E. 269]

We have substituted sophistication for superstition, at least measurably so. But the sophistication is often as irrational and as much at the mercy of words as the superstition it replaces.   [E.N. 44]

Apart from conversation, from discourse and communication, there is no thought and no meaning, only just events, dumb, preposterous, destructive.   [C.E. 129]

The naturalistic method, when it is consistently followed, destroys many things once cherished; but it destroys them by revealing their inconsistency with the nature of things—a flaw that always attended them and deprived them of efficacy for aught save emotional consolation. But its main purport is not destructive; empirical naturalism is rather a winnowing fan.   [E.N. iii]

Men readily persuade themselves that they are devoted to intellectual certainty for its own sake. Actually they want it because of its bearing on safeguarding what they desire and esteem.   [Q.C. 39]

By reading the characteristic features of any man's castles in the air you can make a shrewd guess as to his underlying desires which are frustrated. . . . Time and memory are true artists; they remold reality nearer to the heart's desire.   [R.P. 104]

The word "relativity" is used as a scarecrow to frighten away philosophers from critical assault upon "absolutisms."   [P.M. 12]

Many of the things we called thoughts were asylums for laziness.   [C.E. 820]

Scientifically the widespread acceptance of an idea seems to testify to custom rather than to truth; prejudice is strengthened in influence, but hardly in value, by the number who share it; conceit is none the less self-conceit because it turns the heads of many.   [E.L. 203]

Only the peculiar hypnotic effect exercised by exclusive preoccupation with knowledge could have led thinkers to identify experience with reception of sensations, when five minutes' observation of a child would have disclosed that sensations count only as stimuli and registers of motor activity expended in doing things.   [Q.C. 156]

To the being fully alive, the future is not ominous but a promise; it surrounds the present as a halo.

[A.E. 18]

Nothing is gained by deliberate effort to return to ideas which have become incredible, and to symbols which have been emptied of their content of obvious meaning. Nothing can be gained by moves which will increase confusion and obscurity, which tend to an emotional hypocrisy and to a phrasemongering or formulae which seem to mean one thing and really import the opposite.   [C.E. 507]

Continued progress in knowledge is the only sure way of protecting old knowledge from degeneration into dogmatic doctrines received on authority, or from imperceptible decay into superstition and old wives' tales.
[R.P. 34]

The common fact that we prize in porportion to rarity has a good deal to do with the exclusive esteem in which knowledge has been held.   [Q.C. 297–8]

Science

The ... revival of genuine science undoubtedly drew stimulus and inspiration from the products of Greek thought. But these products were reanimated by contact and interaction with just the things of ordinary experience and the instruments of use in practical arts which in classic Greek thought were supposed to contaminate the purity of science.   [L. 74]

The scientific attitude may almost be defined as that which is capable of enjoying the doubtful; scientific method is, in one aspect, a technique for making a productive use of doubt by converting it into operations of definite inquiry.   [Q.C. 228]

Knowledge falters when imagination clips its wings or fears to use them. Every great advance in science has issued from a new audacity of imagination.
[Q.C. 310]

As long as we worship science and are afraid of philosophy we shall have no great science; we shall have a lagging and halting continuation of what is thought and said elsewhere.   [P.C. 12]

Without systematic formulation of ruling ideas, inquiry is kept in the domain of opinion and action in the realm of conflict.   [L. 508]

The history of science ... shows that the verifiability (as positivism understands it) of hypotheses is not nearly as important as is their directive power.

[L. 519]

It is very easy for science to be regarded as a guarantee that goes with the sale of goods rather than as a light to the eyes and a lamp to the feet. It is prized for its prestige value rather than as an organ of personal illumination and liberation.   [S.S.E. 15–16]

Since scientific methods simply exhibit free intelligence operating in the best manner available at a given time, the cultural waste, confusion, and distortion that result from the failure to use these methods, in all fields in connection with all problems, is incalculable.

[L. 535]

The neutrality of science to the uses made of it renders it silly to talk about its bankruptcy, or to worship it as the usherer in of a new age.   [P.C. 320]

Seeming exceptions to law or general principle ("accidents" in the old sense) are now the nutriment upon which scientific inquiry feeds.   [L. 138]

Surely there is no more significant question before the world than this question of the possibility and method of reconciliation of the attitudes of practical science and contemplative esthetic appreciation. Without the former, man will be the sport and victim of natural forces which he cannot use or control. Without the latter, mankind might become a race of economic monsters, restlessly driving hard bargains with nature and with one another, bored with leisure or capable of putting it to use only in ostentatious display and extravagant dissipation.   [R.P. 127]

Instead of science eliminating ends and inquiries controlled by teleological considerations, it has, on the contrary, enormously freed and expanded activity and thought in telic matters. . . . Multitudes of new qualities have been brought into existence by the applications of physical science, and, what is even more important, our power to bring qualities within actual experience, when we so desire, has been intensified almost beyond the possibility of estimate.   [L. 78]

Factual science may collect statistics and make charts. But its predictions are, as has been well said, but past history reversed.   [A.E. 346]

Man, a child in understanding of himself, has placed in his hands physical tools of incalculable power. He plays with them like a child. . . . The instrumentality becomes a master and works fatally . . . not because it has a will but because man has not.   [P.P. 175]

Insistence upon numerical measurement, when it is not inherently required by the consequence to be effected, is a mark of respect for the ritual of scientific practice at the expense of its substance.   [L. 205]

The abstractions of mathematics and physics represent the common denominators in all things experienceable. Taken by themselves they seem to present a *caput mortuum*. Erected into complete statements of reality as such, they become hallucinatory obsessions.   [Q.C. 218]

Popular psychology is a mass of cant, of slush, and of superstition worthy of the most flourishing days of the medicine man.   [P.P. 165]

It is only the worn-out cynic, the devitalized sensualist, and the fanatical dogmatist who interpret the continuous change of science as proving that, since each successive statement is wrong, the whole record is error and folly; and that the present truth is only the error not yet found out.   [E.L. 101–02]

Facts and Values

The problem of restoring integration and co-operation between man's beliefs about the world in which he lives and his beliefs about the values and purposes that should direct his conduct is the deepest problem of modern life.   [Q.C. 255]

We live . . . in a state of divided allegiance. In outward activities and current enjoyments, we are frenetically absorbed in mundane affairs in ways which, if they were formulated for intellectual acceptance, would be repudiated as low and unworthy. [Q.C. 77]

Individuals vibrate between a past that is intellectually too empty to give stability and a present that is too diversely crowded and chaotic to afford balance or direction to ideas and emotion.   [I.O. 52–53]

What will it profit a man to do this, that, and the other specific thing, if he has no clear idea of why he is doing them, no clear idea of the way they bear upon actual conditions and of the end to be reached?   [E.T. 302]

The term "ideal" has been cheapened by sentimental popular use, and by use in philosophic discourse for apologetic purposes to disguise discords and cruelties in existence.   [A.E. 185]

Not all who say *Ideals, Ideals*, shall enter the kingdom of the ideal, but only those shall enter who know and who respect the roads that conduct to the kingdom.
[C.E. 442]

Ideals are held up to follow; standards are given to work by; laws are provided to guide action. . . . If they cannot do this, not merely by accident, but of their own intrinsic nature, they are worse than inert. They are impudent impostors and logical self-contradictions.
[E.E. 162]

When we take means for ends we indeed fall into moral materialism. But when we take ends without regard to means we degenerate into sentimentalism. In the name of the ideal we fall back upon mere luck and chance and magic or exhortation and preaching; or else upon a fanaticism that will force the realization of preconceived ends at any cost.   [R.P. 73]

Poetry, art, religion are precious things. They cannot be maintained by lingering in the past and futilely wishing to restore what the movement of events in science, industry, and politics has destroyed.   [R.P. 212]

Our idealism will never prosper until it rests upon the organization and resolute use of the greater forces of modern life: industry, commerce, finance, scientific inquiry and discussion and the actualities of human companionship.   [C.E. 635]

The fact that something is desired only raises the *question* of its desirability; it does not settle it. Only a child in the degree of his immaturity thinks to settle the question of desirability by reiterated proclamation: "I want it, I want it, I want it."   [Q.C. 260]

It is simply these active powers getting off and looking at themselves to see what they are like; to see what they are upon the whole, permanently, in their final bearings, and not simply as they are at the moment and in their relative isolation. The ideal, in other words, is the self-consciousness of the impulse.   [E.E. 110]

Values are as unstable as the forms of clouds. The things that possess them are exposed to all the contingencies of existence, and they are indifferent to our likings and tastes. Good things change and vanish not only with changes in the environing medium but with changes in ourselves.   [E.N. 399]

It would presumably be taken as a sign of extreme naïveté, if not of callous insensitiveness, if one were to ask why all this ardor to reconcile the findings of natural science with the validity of values. Why should any increase of knowledge seem like a threat to what we prize, admire, and approve? Why should we not proceed to employ our gains in science to improve our judgments about values, and to regulate our actions so as to make values more secure and more widely shared in existence?

[Q.C. 42]

Morality

It is a piece of scholasticism to suppose that a moral rule has its own self-defining and self-applying content. What truth-telling, what honesty, what patience, what self-respect are, changes . . . with every added insight into the relations of men and things. It is only the breath of intelligence blowing through such rules that keeps them from the putrefaction which awaits all barren idealities.

[P.D. 317]

Morals is not a catalogue of acts nor a set of rules to be applied like drugstore prescriptions or cookbook recipes. The need in morals is for specific methods of inquiry and of contrivance.   [R.P. 169–70]

Ready-made rules available at a moment's notice for settling any kind of moral difficulty . . . have been the chief object of the ambition of moralists. In the much less complicated and less changing matters of bodily health such pretensions are known as quackery.

[H.N.C. 238]

Where there is no activity having a growing significance, appeal to principle is either purely verbal, or a form of obstinate pride, or an appeal to extraneous considerations clothed with a dignified title.   [D.E. 410]

A man who prides himself upon acting upon principle is likely to be a man who insists upon having his own way without learning from experience what is the better way.   [D.E. 410]

Moral principles that exalt themselves by degrading human nature are in effect committing suicide.
[H.N.C. 2]

Conventional morality is a drab morality, in which the only fatal thing is to be conspicuous.
[H.N.C. 4]

The chief practical effect of refusing to recognize the connection of custom with moral standards is to deify some special custom and treat it as eternal, immutable, outside of criticism and revision.   [H.N.C. 81]

What is termed spiritual culture has usually been futile, with something rotten about it, just because it has been conceived as a thing which a man might have internally—and therefore exclusively.   [D.E. 143]

Let us perfect ourselves within, and in due season changes in society will come of themselves, is the teaching. And while saints are engaged in introspection, burly sinners run the world.   [R.P. 196]

If at a critical juncture the moving force of events is always too much for conscience, the remedy is not to deplore the wickedness of those who manipulate events. Such a conscience is largely self-conceit. The remedy is to connect conscience with the forces that are moving in another direction. Then will conscience itself have compulsive power instead of being forever the martyred and the coerced.   [C.E. 580]

"Charity" may even be used as a means for administering a sop to one's social conscience while at the same time it buys off the resentment which might otherwise grow up in those who suffer from social injustice.   [E. 334]

It is only as our ideas about morals ... become part of the working behavior of the mind towards its concrete duties, that they are other than curiosities for the collector of the bric-a-brac of thought.   [P.D. 317]

When physics, chemistry, biology, medicine, contribute to the detection of concrete human woes and to the development of plans for remedying them and relieving the human estate, they become moral; they become part of the apparatus of moral inquiry or science. The latter then loses its peculiar flavor of the didactic and pedantic; its ultra-moralistic and hortatory tone. It loses its thinness and shrillness as well as its vagueness. [R.P. 173]

No ends are accomplished without the use of force. It is consequently no presumption against a measure, political, international, jural, economic, that it involves a use of force. Squeamishness about force is the mark not of idealistic but of moonstruck morals. [C.E. 787]

Men have never fully used the powers they possess to advance the good in life, because they have waited upon some power external to themselves and to nature to do the work they are responsible for doing. [C.F. 46]

I have little patience with those who are so anxious to save their influence for some important crisis that they never risk its use in any present emergency.

[C.E. 584]

We are all natural Jack Horners. If the plum comes when we put in and pull out our thumb we attribute the satisfactory result to personal virtue. The plum is obtained, and it is not easy to distinguish obtaining from attaining, acquisition from achieving.   [H.N.C. 253]

The man who feels that *his* virtues are his own personal accomplishments is likely to be also the one who thinks that by passing laws he can throw the fear of God into others and make them virtuous by edict and prohibitory mandate.   [H.N.C. 27]

Men will never love their enemies until they cease to have enmities.   [Q.C. 308]

What is sometimes called a benevolent interest in others may be but an unwitting mask for an attempt to dictate to them what their good shall be, instead of an endeavor to free them so that they may seek and find the good of their own choice.   [D.E. 141]

But persons who profess no regard for happiness as a test of action have an unfortunate way of living up to their principle by making others *un*happy.   [G.P. 58]

The badness of good people . . . is the revenge taken by human nature for the injuries heaped upon it in the name of morality.   [H.N.C. 4]

Toleration is thus not just an attitude of good-humored indifference. It is positive willingness to permit reflection and inquiry to go on in the faith that the truly right will be rendered more secure through questioning and discussion, while things which have endured merely from custom will be amended or done away with.   [E. 252]

Conceit looks through the wrong end of a telescope and minimizes the significance possessed by objects in favor of the alleged importance of the self.   [A.E. 104]

If you know what sort of things a man finds enjoyable and disagreeable you have a sure clew to his nature—and the principle applies to ourselves as well as to others.   [E. 210]

Art

Art . . . is more than a stir of energy in the doldrums of the dispirited, or a calm in the storms of the troubled. Through art, meanings of objects that are otherwise dumb, inchoate, restricted, and resisted are clarified and concentrated, and not by thought working laboriously upon them, nor by escape into a world of mere sense, but by creation of a new experience. [A.E. 132–3]

Art has been the means of keeping alive the sense of purposes that outrun evidence and of meanings that transcend indurated habit. [A.E. 348]

Philosophy is said to begin in wonder and end in understanding. Art departs from what has been understood and ends in wonder. In this end, the human contribution in art is also the quickened work of nature in man.

[A.E. 270]

The imagination, by means of art, makes a concession to sense in employing its materials, but nevertheless uses sense to suggest underlying ideal truth. Art is thus a way of having the substantial cake of reason while also enjoying the sensuous pleasure of eating it.   [A.E. 258]

In the end, works of art are the only media of complete and unhindered communication between man and man that can occur in a world full of gulfs and walls that limit community of experience.   [A.E. 105]

For arts that are merely useful are not arts but routines; and arts that are merely final are not arts but passive amusements and distractions, different from other indulgent dissipations only in dependence upon a certain acquired refinement or "cultivation."   [E.N. 361]

Buildings, among all art objects, come the nearest to expressing the stability and endurance of existence. They are to mountains what music is to the sea. Because of its inherent power to endure, architecture records and celebrates more than any other art the generic features of our common human life.   [A.E. 230]

The art of literature . . . works with loaded dice; its material is charged with meanings they have absorbed through immemorial time. Its material thus has an intellectual force superior to that of any other art, while it equals the capacity of architecture to present the values of collective life.   [A.E. 239–40]

There are . . . matters which lend themselves naturally to poetry, and where a vesture of emotion and imagination is favorable to the apprehension of the meanings involved. . . . Only crude, illiterate Philistinism will insist upon translating poetic symbolism into the prose of the first reader.   [C.E. 454–55]

"Imagination" shares with "beauty" the doubtful honor of being the chief theme in esthetic writings of enthusiastic ignorance.   [A.E. 267]

Esthetic theories are filled with fossils of antiquated psychologies and are overlaid with débris of psychological controversies.   [A.E. 245]

As long as art is the beauty parlor of civilization, neither art nor civilization is secure.   [A.E. 344]

Religion

Any activity pursued in behalf of an ideal end against obstacles and in spite of threats of personal loss because of conviction of its general and enduring value is religious in quality.   [C.F. 27]

Faith in the continued disclosing of truth through directed co-operative human endeavor is more religious in quality than is any faith in a completed revelation.
[C.F. 26]

Within the flickering inconsequential acts of separate selves dwells a sense of the whole which claims and dignifies them. In its presence we put off mortality and live in the universal. The life of the community in which we live and have our being is the fit symbol of this relationship. The acts in which we express our perception of the ties which bind us to others are its only rites and ceremonies.
[H.N.C. 331–32]

Instead of marking the freedom and peace of the individual as a member of an infinite whole, it [religion] has been petrified into a slavery of thought and sentiment, as intolerant superiority on the part of the few and an intolerable burden on the part of the many.   [H.N.C. 331]

Our Christianity has become identified with vague feeling and with an optimism which we think is a sign of a pious faith in Providence but which in reality is a trust in luck, a deification of the feeling of success regardless of any intelligent discrimination of the nature of success.

[C.E. 634]

Intellectually, religious emotions are not creative but conservative. They attach themselves readily to the current view of the world and consecrate it. They steep and dye intellectual fabrics in the seething vat of emotions; they do not form their warp and woof.   [I.D. 2–3]

Contempt for nature is understandable, at least historically; even though it seems both intellectually petty and morally ungracious to feel contempt for the matrix of our being and the inescapable condition of our lives.

[I.O. 97]

Social Philosophy

The measure of civilization is the degree in which the method of co-operative intelligence replaces the method of brute conflict.   [L.S.A. 81]

We have talked a great deal about democracy, and now for the first time we have to make an effort to find out what it is.   [C.E. 725]

The foundation of democracy is faith in the capacities of human nature; faith in human intelligence and in the power of pooled and co-operative experience. It is not belief that these things are complete but that, if given a show, they will grow and be able to generate progressively the knowledge and wisdom needed to guide collective action.

[P.M. 59]

Democracy . . . denotes . . . aristocracy carried to its limit. It is a claim that every human being as an individual may be the best for some particular purpose and hence be the most fitted to rule, to lead, in that specific respect.   [C.E. 489]

The keynote of democracy as a way of life may be expressed, it seems to me, as the necessity for the participation of every mature human being in formation of the values that regulate the living of men together: which is necessary from the standpoint of both the general social welfare and the full development of human beings as individuals.

[P.M. 58]

The prime condition of a democratically organized public is a kind of knowledge and insight which does not yet exist.   [P.P. 166]

The spread of literacy, the immense extension of the influence of the press in books, newspapers, periodicals, make the issue peculiarly urgent for a democracy. The very agencies that a century and a half ago were looked upon as those that were sure to advance the cause of democratic freedom, are those which now make it possible to create pseudo-public opinion and to undermine democracy from within.   [F.C. 148]

It is quite possible that in the long run . . . the greatest foe to freedom of thought and expression is not those who fear such freedom because of its possible effect upon their own standing and fortune, but is the triviality and irrelevancy of the ideas that are entertained, and the futile and perhaps corrupting way in which they are expressed.

[I.M.W. 723–24]

Mankind was ever subject to passion, dogma, self-interest, partisanship, and propaganda. But these causes have lost whatever frank, stout downrightness they once possessed. . . . They find entrance into the mind invested with a protective sheen of loyalty, sanity and security, progress, or whatever ideals are in fashion.   [E.T. 185]

Democracy cannot flourish where the chief influences in selecting subject matter of instruction are utilitarian ends narrowly conceived for the masses, and, for the higher education of the few, the traditions of a specialized cultivated class.   [D.E. 226]

The serious threat to our democracy is not the existence of foreign totalitarian states. It is the existence within our own personal attitudes and within our own institutions of conditions similar to those which have given a victory to external authority, discipline, uniformity, and dependence upon The Leader in foreign countries.

[F.C. 49]

A society of free individuals in which all, through their own work, contribute to the liberation and enrichment of the lives of others, is the only environment in which any individual can really grow normally to his full stature.   [E.T. 298]

To profess democracy as an ultimate ideal and the suppression of democracy as a means to the ideal may be possible in a country that has never known even rudimentary democracy, but when professed in a country that has anything of a genuine democratic spirit in its traditions, it signifies desire for possession and retention of power by a class, whether that class be called Fascist or Proletarian.

[L.S.A. 86]

People love to stand on their heads intellectually, and so it is that the Marxians who have given the world its best modern demonstration of the power of ideas and of intellectual leadership, are the ones who most deny that these things have any efficacy.   [C.E. 155]

Literary persons have been chiefly the ones in this country who have fallen for Marxist theory, since they are the ones who, having the least amount of scientific attitude, swallow most readily the notion that "science" is a new kind of infallibility.   [F.C. 96]

This conversion of abstractions into entities smells more of a dialectic of concepts than of a realistic examination of facts, even though it makes more of an emotional appeal to many than do the results of the latter.

[L.S.A. 80]

Doctrines . . . which assume that because certain ends are desirable therefore those ends and nothing else will result from the use of force to attain them are but another example of the limitations put upon intelligence by any absolute theory.   [P.M. 139]

The feeling that social change of any basic character can be brought about only by violent force is the product of lack of faith in intelligence as a method, and this loss of faith is in large measure the product of a schooling that . . . has not enabled youth to face intelligently the realities of our social life, political and economic.

[P.M. 78–79]

Nothing is blinder than the supposition that we live in a society and world so static that either nothing new will happen or else it will happen because of the use of violence. Social change is here as a fact.   [L.S.A. 56]

Insistence that the use of violent force is *inevitable* limits the use of available intelligence. . . . Commitment to inevitability is always the fruit of dogma; intelligence does not pretend to *know* save as a result of experimentation. . . . Moreover, acceptance in advance of the inevitability of violence tends to produce the use of violence in cases where peaceful methods might otherwise avail.

[L.S.A. 78]

The only ones who have the right to criticize "radicals" . . . are those who put as much effort into reconstruction as the rebels are putting into destruction.

[H.N.C. 167–68]

The ultimate problem of production is the production of human beings. To this end, the production of goods is intermediate and auxiliary.   [I.N.W. 430]

It is possible to regard the present emphasis upon economic factors as a sort of intellectual revenge taken upon its earlier all but total neglect.   [F.C. 14]

There is a subterranean partnership between those who employ the existing economic order for selfish pecuniary gain and those who turn their backs upon it in the interest of personal complacency, private dignity, and irresponsibility.   [I.O. 158–59]

The new industrialism was largely the old feudalism, living in a bank instead of a castle and brandishing the check of credit instead of the sword.

[H.N.C. 213]

Our reward of industry and thrift is so accurately adjusted to individual ability that it is natural and proper that the workers should look forward with dread to the age of fifty or fifty-five, when they will be laid on the shelf.   [I.O. 11]

Nothing gives us Americans the horrors more than to hear that some misguided creature in some low part of the earth preaches what we practice—and practice much more efficiently than anyone else—namely, economic determinism.   [I.O. 13]

The only hope for liberalism is to surrender ... the doctrine that liberty is a full-fledged ready-made possession of individuals independent of social institutions and arrangements, and to realize that social control, especially of economic forces, is necessary in order to render secure the liberties of the individual, including civil liberties.
[P.M. 121]

The slogans of the liberalism of one period often become the bulwarks of reaction in a subsequent era.
[P.C. 139]

The social situation has been so changed by the factors of an industrial age that traditional general principles have little practical meaning. They persist as emotional cries rather than as reasoned ideas.   [P.P. 133]

Men hoist the banner of the ideal, and then march in the direction that concrete conditions suggest and reward.   [Q.C. 281]

We confused rapidity of change with advance, and we took certain gains in our own comfort and ease as signs that cosmic forces were working inevitably to improve the whole state of human affairs. Having reaped where we had not sown, our undisciplined imaginations installed in the heart of history forces which were to carry on progress whether or no, and whose advantages we were progressively to enjoy.   [C.E. 820–21]

The doctrine of evolution has been popularily used to give a kind of cosmic sanction to the notion of an automatic and wholesale progress in human affairs. Our part, the human part, was simply to enjoy the usufruct. Evolution inherited all the goods of Divine Providence and had the advantage of being in fashion. Even a great and devastating war is not too great a price to pay for such an infantile and selfish dream.   [P.D. 462]

Let us admit the case of the conservative; if we once start thinking, no one can guarantee where we shall come out, except that many objects, ends, and institutions are surely doomed. Every thinker puts some portion of an apparently stable world in peril and no one can wholly predict what will emerge in its place.   [E.N. 222]

If one stops to consider the matter, is there not something strange in the fact that men should consider loyalty to "laws," principles, standards, ideals, to be an inherent virtue, accounted unto them for righteousness? It is as if they were making up for some secret sense of weakness by rigidity and intensity of insistent attachment.

[Q.C. 278]

The notion that laws govern and forces rule is an animistic survival. It is a product of reading nature in terms of politics in order to turn around and then read politics in the light of supposed sanctions of nature.

[I.D. 72]

For in higher practical matters we still live in dread of change and of problems. Like men of olden time—with respect to natural phenomena—we prefer to accept and endure or to enjoy . . . what we find in possession of the field, and at most, to arrange it under concepts, and thus give it the form of rationality.   [Q.C. 101]

Natural rights and natural liberties exist only in the kingdom of mythological social zoölogy.

[L.S.A. 17]

It is human nature to think along the easiest lines, and this induces men when they want conspicuous leaders in the civil function to fasten upon those who are already conspicuous, no matter what the reason.   [P.P. 79]

No government by experts in which the masses do not have the chance to inform the experts as to their needs can be anything but an oligarchy managed in the interests of the few. And the enlightenment must proceed in ways which force the administrative specialists to take account of the needs. The world has suffered more from leaders and authorities than from the masses.   [P.P. 208]

The madness with which the gods afflict those whom they would destroy is precisely the temptation to use a temporary possession of strategic power so as to make that power permanent.   [C.E. 816]

In modern wars, anger and hatred come after the war has started; they are effects of war, not the cause of it.   [P.M. 187]

The vehement conviction of each warring nation of the absolute righteousness of its own cause is the whistling of children in the awful unexpectedness of a graveyard.   [C.E. 131–32]

The undisguised scramble after the [World War I] armistice days reminded us of the Fall of Man, and we hurried back into our Paradise, though remaining on the lookout for remunerative investments in the outer world of sin and misery.   [C.E. 616]

There is something strange in the history of toleration. Almost all men have learned the lesson of toleration with respect to past heresies and divisions.   [C.E. 567]

It has often been assumed that freedom of speech, oral and written, is independent of freedom of thought, and that you cannot take the latter away in any case, since it goes on inside of minds where it cannot be got at. No idea could be more mistaken. . . . If ideas when aroused cannot be communicated, they either fade away or become warped and morbid.   [P.C. 297]

To explain the origin of the state by saying that man is a political animal is to travel in a verbal circle.
[P.P. 9]

By various agencies, unintentional and designed, a society transforms uninitiated and seemingly alien beings into robust trustees of its own resources and ideals.
[D.E. 12]

Custom consolidates what accident may have originated.   [P.P. 80]

Our State is founded on freedom, but when we train the State of tomorrow, we allow it just as little freedom as possible.   [S.T. 304]

When customs are flexible and youth is educated as youth and not as premature adulthood, no nation grows old.   [H.N.C. 102]

Classic political science . . . becomes a recluse from the world of affairs and alternates between a pedantic conservatism and a complacent acceptance of any brute change which happens, if only a decent time be allowed to elapse.   [C.E. 730]

All intelligent political criticism is comparative. It deals not with all-or-none situations, but with practical alternatives; an absolutistic indiscriminate attitude, whether in praise or blame, testifies to the heat of feeling rather than the light of thought.   [P.P. 110]

If the growth of the free mind to fullness of stature and social recognition was to have been prevented, it should have been strangled at birth. It is now too late. Hostile influences may and will deflect and retard its progress. Individuals will be annoyed and suffer harm. But the spirit of thought and inquiry will never be beaten by weapons of flesh and blood.   [E.T. 197]

Fidelity to the nature to which we belong, as parts however weak, demands that we cherish our desires and ideals till we have converted them into intelligence. . . . When we have used our thought to its utmost and have thrown into the moving unbalanced balance of things our puny strength, we know that though the universe slay us still we may trust, for our lot is one with whatever is good in existence. We know that such thought and effort is one condition of the coming into existence of the better.

[P.D. 553]

Education

The first act evoked by a genuine faith in education is a conviction of sin and act of repentance as to the institutions and methods which we now call educational.

[E.T. 149]

The inert, stupid quality of current customs perverts learning into a willingness to follow where others point-the way, into conformity, constriction, surrender of skepticism and experiment. . . . We think of the insolent coercions, the insinuating briberies, the pedagogic solemnities by which the freshness of youth can be faded and its vivid curiosities dulled. Education becomes the art of taking advantage of the helplessness of the young. [H.N.C. 64]

It would not be wholly palatable to have to face the actual psychological condition of the majority of the pupils that leave our schools. [E.E. 87]

It [the traditional school] is arranged on the fatal plan of a hothouse, forcing to a sterile show, rather than fostering all-around growth. It does not foster an individuality capable of an enduring resistance and of creative activities. [S.T. 18]

Our schools send out men meeting the exigencies of contemporary life clothed in the chain armor of antiquity, and priding themselves on the awkwardness of their movements as evidences of deep-wrought, time-tested convictions.   [C.E. 779–80]

The pupil must learn what has meaning, what enlarges his horizon, instead of mere trivialities. He must become acquainted with truths, instead of things that were regarded as such fifty years ago, or that are taken as interesting by the misunderstanding of a partially educated teacher.   [S.S. 93]

The school cannot be a preparation for social life excepting as it reproduces, within itself, the typical conditions of social life.   [E.E. 34]

Culture, if it is to be genuine and educative, and not an external polish or factitious varnish, represents the vital union of information and discipline. It designates the socialization of the individual in his whole outlook upon life and mode of dealing with it.   [E.E. 45]

Unless culture be a superficial polish, a veneering of mahogany over common wood, it surely is this —the growth of the imagination in flexibility, in scope, and in sympathy, till the life which the individual lives is informed with the life of nature and of society.   [S.S. 73]

A method is ethically defective that, while giving the child a glibness in the mechanical facility of reading, leaves him at the mercy of suggestion and chance environment to decide whether he reads the "yellow journal," the trashy novel, or the literature which inspires and makes more valid his whole life.   [E.E. 153]

The profit of education is the ability it gives to discriminate, to make distinctions that penetrate below the surface.   One may not be able to lay hold of the realities beneath the froth and foam, but at least one who is educated does not take the latter to be the realities; one knows that there is a difference between sound and sense, between what is emphatic and what is distinctive, between what is conspicuous and what is important.   [C.E. 776]

Education must have a tendency . . . to form attitudes. The tendency to form attitudes which will express themselves in intelligent social action is something very different from indoctrination, just as taking intelligent aim is very different from firing BB shot in the air at random with the kind of vague, pious hope that somehow or other a bird may fly into some of the shot.   [P.M. 55–56]

It is as if no one could be educated in the full sense until everyone is developed beyond the reach of prejudice, stupidity, and apathy.   [P.D. 380]

The schools have . . . the responsibility of seeing to it that those who leave its walls have ideas that are worth thinking and worth being expressed, as well as having the courage to express them against the opposition of reactionaries and standpatters.   [I.M.W. 723]

The mistake of making the records and remains of the past the main material of education is that it cuts the vital connection of present and past, and tends to make the past a rival of the present and the present a more or less futile imitation of the past. Under such circumstances, culture becomes an ornament and solace; a refuge and an asylum. Men escape from the crudities of the present to live in its imagined refinements, instead of using what the past offers as an agency for ripening these crudities.

[D.E. 88]

Knowledge is humanistic in quality not because it is *about* human products in the past, but because of what it *does* in liberating human intelligence and human sympathy. Any subject matter which accomplishes this result is humane, and any subject matter which does not accomplish it is not even educational.   [D.E. 269]

Our dominant conception of discipline is a travesty; there is only one genuine discipline, namely, that which takes effect in producing habits of observation and judgment that insure intelligent desires.   [P.C. 289–90]

A truly liberal, and liberating, education would refuse today to isolate vocational training on any of its levels from a continuous education in the social, moral, and scientific contexts within which wisely administered callings and professions must function.   [P.M. 146]

It is not the subject *per se* that is educative or that is conducive to growth. There is no subject that is in and of itself, or without regard to the stage of growth attained by the learner, such that inherent educational value can be attributed to it.   [I.M.W. 671]

Discipline is a product, an outcome, an achievement, not something applied from without. All genuine education *terminates* in discipline, but it *proceeds* by engaging the mind in activities worth while for their own sake.
[H.W.T. 86–87]

There is no doubt that the ability to perform an irksome duty is a very useful accomplishment, but the usefulness does not lie in the irksomeness of the task. Things are not useful or necessary because they are unpleasant or tiresome, but in spite of these characteristics.
[S.T. 299–300]

It will be found true, as a general principle, that whenever any study which was originally utilitarian in purpose becomes useless because of a change in conditions, it is retained as a necessary educational ornament (as useless buttons are retained on the sleeves of men's coats) or else because it is so useless that it must be fine for mental discipline.   [E.T. 126–27]

Most of . . . children's alleged native egoism is simply an egoism which runs counter to an adult's egoism. To a grown-up person who is too absorbed in his own affairs to take an interest in children's affairs, children doubtless seem unreasonably engrossed in *their* own affairs.

[D.E. 52]

Normal child and normal adult alike . . . are engaged in growing. . . . With respect to the development of powers devoted to coping with specific scientific and economic problems we may say the child should be growing in manhood. With respect to sympathetic curiosity, unbiased responsiveness, and openness of mind, we may say that the adult should be growing in childlikeness.   [D.E. 59]

The public school is the willing pack horse of our social system; it is the true hero of the refrain: Let George do it.   [C.E. 474]

The schools are a drift rather than a system.
[P.M. 89]

Investigators and teachers . . . , being human, may substitute dogmas for hypotheses, mistake propaganda for teaching, novelty for depth, and the very subjects that most need free inquiry and that may most readily excite intellectual interest in young people become subject to a kind of perversion, influential in the measure of its vague intangibility.   [E.T. 195]

Teaching may be compared to selling commodities. No one can sell unless someone buys. We should ridicule a merchant who said that he had sold a great many goods although no one had bought any. But perhaps there are teachers who think that they have done a good day's teaching irrespective of what pupils have learned.
[H.W.T. 35]

The gullibility of specialized scholars when out of their own lines, their extravagant habits of inference and speech, their ineptness in reaching conclusions in practical matters, their egotistical engrossment in their own subjects, are extreme examples of the bad effects of severing studies completely from their ordinary connections in life.
[H.W.T. 62]

In the degree in which our colleges are not liberal, it is because the spirit of the American communal scene is dense, given to both cocksureness and conformity, prone to sudden and short-time excitements, shifty, in love with immediate and showy success, addicted to a savage-like alternation between adoration of fetishes and whipping them.   [E.T. 188]

Display, the adornment of person, the kind of social companionship and entertainment which give prestige, and the spending of money, have been made into definite callings. Unconsciously to themselves the higher institutions of learning have been made to contribute to preparation for these employments.   [D.E. 365]

The net result of the alterations produced by the social changes . . . has been to render the name "liberal arts college" reminiscent rather than descriptive when it is applied to many of our collegiate institutions.   [P.M. 86]

Withdrawal from the hard and fast and narrow contents of the old curriculum is only the negative side of the matter. If we do not go on and go far in the positive direction of providing a body of subject matter much richer, more varied and flexible, and also in truth more definite, judged in terms of the experience of those being educated, . . . we shall tend to leave an educational vacuum in which anything may happen.   [E.T. 294]

What the best and wisest parent wants for his own child, that must the community want for all of its children.   [S.S. 19]

Education is not something to be forced upon children and youth from without, but is the growth of capacities with which human beings are endowed at birth.

[S.T. 2]

The child's own instincts and powers furnish the material and give the starting-point for all education.

[E.T. 4]

The need for taking account of spontaneous and uncoerced interest and activity is a genuine need; but without care and thought it results, all too readily, in a detached multiplicity of isolated short-time activities or projects, and the continuity necessary for growth is lost.

[E.T. 295]

Deification of childish whim, unripened fancy, and arbitrary emotion is certainly a piece of pure romanticism. The would-be reformers who emphasize out of due proportion and perspective these aspects of the principle of individualism betray their own cause.   [E.T. 69]

Utilizing of interest and habit to make of it something fuller, wider, something more refined and under better control, might be defined as the teacher's whole duty.

[E.E. 126]

This does not mean that the textbook must disappear, but that its function is changed. It becomes a guide for the pupil by which he may economize time and mistakes. The teacher and the book are no longer the only instructors; the hands, the eyes, the ears, in fact the whole body, become sources of information, while teacher and textbook become respectively the starter and the tester.

[S.T. 74]

The result of the educative process is capacity for further education.　[D.E. 79]